Acclaim for *Keep the Curls*

**"...the ultimate "Do-It-Yourself" book for women
who desire to flourish in today's world."**

---

*Crystal Langdon has written the ultimate "Do-It-Yourself"
book for women who desire to flourish in today's world.
Keep the Curls is a thoughtful manual about life, faith, and
becoming your best.*

—Sandra J. Albano,
CCO / Finance & Operations Principal
G.A. Repple & Company,
Reg. Broker/Dealer & Investment Advisor

"She presents only what she practices and teaches only what she lives: nurturing, overcoming, fulfilled femininity."

I have known the author for many years. She is the real deal, authentic in every way. Crystal Langdon is the genuine article. Her long-term marriage is strong, her children are exceptional, and her business is prosperous. She presents only what she practices and teaches only what she lives: nurturing, overcoming, fulfilled femininity.

—C. A. Elmore
Chief Information Officer and Special Assistant
to the President
Inspiration Networks, Inc.

"...coaxing us to acknowledge our worth without merchandizing our lives..."

The world has never given proper credit to the value of women in the marketplace. Crystal Langdon shows us the broad perspective of ourselves as women. Crystal gives a heartfelt understanding of each woman's precious identity, coaxing us to acknowledge our worth without merchandizing our lives away by becoming what we are not. Walk into this book with your shoulders back and embrace Crystal's discovery of your "CEO DNA Code." You will undoubtedly come to understand that you are more important than ever before in the history of womankind. What an enlightenment and a "crystal clear" view of freedom!

—Irene Joy Anderson, CFO Standsure

"I have consulted and coached entrepreneurs for years and how I needed this wonderful resource!"

I have consulted and coached entrepreneurs for years and how I needed this wonderful resource! Keep the Curls *is an essential resource for every husband and wife, business executive or manager, as well as every woman seeking to maximize her potential and impact at home and in the marketplace.*

—Dr. Larry Keefauver, President of YMCS
Bestselling author and international speaker

"This book is NOT for women only...an explosion of creativity."

This book is NOT for women only, though every woman should certainly read it! Crystal Langdon is the genuine real thing. She is a coming watermark on doing business of all kinds and you find that out on the leaves of her writing. Herein, you'll observe the standards that Crystal personally sets in the business world and how they are quintessential to the rebirth of proper business that is coming upon the world. Put knowledge, wisdom, perceptivity, and a healthy view of what needs to be done together and you experience an explosion of creativity. That is what you get from Crystal—that is what you'll read in the pages of this book or anything that Crystal Langdon writes.

—Wayne C Anderson, President/CEO IAM

> **"...to liberate the gifts within women and help us men understand how to embrace women without being afraid that we will lose our place."**

Crystal Langdon is a woman of action, intentionality, industry, grace, and strength. In this book, she uses her experience and insights as an accomplished business leader to liberate the gifts within women and help us men understand how to embrace women without being afraid that we will lose our place. At a time when male leadership has led our government and corporations to high debt and corruption, here is a book that can unleash a generation of women leaders who can come alongside men to bring the balance and, who knows, maybe take the lead if necessary. A must read for all, especially those aspiring to be game changers.

—Patrice Tsague CSO, NPIM

> **"For too long an unhealthy view of gender roles has dominated the business arena."**

For too long an unhealthy view of gender roles has dominated the business arena. Women and men are created different, but neither gender is better than the other. In Keep the Curls, *Crystal Langdon unlocks the identity crisis that women have struggled with in crossing over from domestic expectations to true marketplace calling. This is a woman who knows of what she speaks. She was born with CEO*

*DNA! Any woman who has held a dream in her heart...
should read this book. It will free you!*

—Tom Michaels Zahradnik
Chief Executive Officer, Sound of Life, Inc.

**"...Crystal challenges women to be set free from the lies
to celebrate their destiny."**

---

*Crystal is a gifted communicator. She challenges women to
be set free from the lies to celebrate their destiny. Women
are CEOs in their marriage, home, business, and community, and are uniquely gifted to multitask as executives in all
of their roles.*

—Glenn Repple
G. A. Repple and Company,
A Registered Broker Dealer & Investment Company

**"...As a man reading this book, I better understand the
natural gifts God built inside the minds and hearts of all
women."**

---

*What a fabulous book! I can't wait to get it into the hands
of all the women in my life, from my wife, my daughter, to
the ladies at my office. As a man reading this book, I better
understand the natural gifts God built inside the minds and
hearts of all women. For believers, this is a modern, practical guide to becoming the virtuous woman described in*

Proverbs 31:10–31. I have known Crystal for many years and have watched her grow professionally. Whatever she does changes lives, and this book is no exception.

—Jeff Armstrong, President
BLA & Kingdom Quest Financial

"...a roadmap for success that should be read by every woman who dreams of owning her own business, and by the men who love and admire them!"

By anyone's standards, Crystal Langdon is a success—as a wife, a mother, and a businesswoman. In this book, Crystal forcefully challenges the cultural myth that to succeed in the marketplace women must sacrifice their femininity on the altars of exploitation and victimization or masculinization. Illustrated by moving glimpses into her personal challenges while serving in her roles as a wife, a mother, and a CEO of her own company, Crystal presents solid evidence that women are gifted for business leadership by virtue of their nurturing nature and their marital and parental experience.

It is my opinion that the challenges of today's world will not be solved without the insight and influence of strong, feminine women who stand as equals beside their male counterparts in the full confidence that they also were born to lead. This book is a roadmap for success that should be read by every woman who dreams of owning her own business, and by the men who love and admire them!

—Richard Carey, Founder/CEO
Lionheart.net

"...a guideline that establishes that women are a much-needed force to be reckoned with, not just in the home, but also in the realm of business."

Keep the Curls *is a success story—not just a guideline for women to succeed in the full-time ministry of the marketplace. It is an inspirational writing that, in truth, is teaching about having a practical future and a hope for making a difference. I would like to encourage you as a reader, to not only read these pages, but to deeply take into your heart the emotions, the fervency, and the motivation that is expressed in this book. It reveals passion, and as we know, it is passion that makes an average person truly successful.*

—Patrick Holloran
President HHIM

Keep the Curls

*Empowering Women
Personally and Professionally*

Crystal Langdon,
Certified Financial Planner™

Keep the Curls
Empowering Women Personally and Professionally
© 2011 Crystal Langdon, Certified Financial Planner™

Securities & Investment Advice through G.A. Repple & Company, A Registered Broker/Dealer and Investment Advisor. Member FINRA/SIPC.

ISBN: 978-0-9847653-3-1

Published by: Crystal Clear Conversations
Crystal Langdon, Certified Financial Planner™
16 The Sage Estates, Suite 301
Albany, NY 12204
(518) 433-7181

Printed in the U.S.A.

Dedications

To my husband:

This book is dedicated to my high school sweetheart, George Langdon IV. You have been a wonderful husband, a great father to our children: protector of our daughters and role model to our son. Thank you for rejoicing in my victories and creating room for me to shine. I have been blessed to have you by my side. You will forever be the spring in my curls!

To my children:

Melonie, you are a woman of great strength and endurance. No physical, emotional, or intellectual obstacle has been able to deter you from living your life by your design. Your strength runs deep and your reservoir of wisdom continues to increase. Keep cultivating your emotional intelligence and equip yourself to release your voice within the governmental spheres, for you have a message the world has yet to hear. You, my precious daughter, are life's game changer. You are the embodiment of all that I had hoped for you to become. I love you.

Stephanie, your name means "Crowned One," and it is evident in all that you do. You are a woman of authority and influence. Your ability to unlock the CEO codes within has allowed you to excel and accomplish more than many will ever attempt in a lifetime. As you hit your stride, you will find yourself before dignitaries and influential decision makers, for you have the ability to open doors bilaterally for those who should be leading and those who have yet to follow!

King George V, my son! You redefine the word "dream!" You break every limitation and boldly challenge all naysayers and obstacles that arise. When you appear on the scene, situations change, hope awakens, and enlargement happens. You are a significant key to unlocking legacy and creating sustainability for subsequent generations to come. So dream on...and dream big!

To my cubs, Brian Paeglow, Justin McMullen, Victoria Persico, Malcolm Chandler, and Kalvin Newsome. Mama and Papa Bear are honored to be a part of your life. We love watching and helping you grow into your destinies!

To my Lord:

Finally, I would be remiss if I did not publicly honor my most intimate counselor, guide, and closest friend: the Lord Jesus Christ. It is He who has endowed me with the ability to articulate and declare an awakening to women throughout this great country and across the world. May I always stay in tune with Your voice and embrace the destiny You have placed within me.

Acknowledgments

To my team at Crystal Clear Finances, thank you for holding the course and providing me with the freedom needed to undertake this project.

To Rachelle Funk, Steve and Carol Knaus, and my sister Jackie…thank you for the many hours spent editing and re-editing!

To IAM, TSH and ALCF for believing in me and providing a platform from which I can roar!

Table of Contents

Introduction

Keep the Curls

As I walked into the room, every head turned. Looks of amusement, disdain, and disinterest caught my eye. I continued to walk forward as I mentally confirmed that my attire was correct, my hair was in place, and that I was in the right room. Confident that nothing was out of place except perhaps me, I adjusted my plastic smile, nodded at the inquiring glances and moved toward the first empty chair I could find.

Their attention on me soon waned and I was able to evaluate the room at leisure. It was another typical business conference. I could see one, two, and then a third non-male person was over in the corner. Including myself, I finally counted a total of four women who had infiltrated this session, crossing "the line" in search of information to help our respective clientele.

As I sat motionless, trying to blend into my chair, I heard the laughter and camaraderie between male colleagues that was clearly reserved for their "invitation-only" conversations. I busied myself with preparing for the speaker and wondered when a room of business professionals would ever consist of more than a 10:1 ratio.

Being a woman in a predominantly male business world was still a battle. For twelve years, I had been attending conferences and business meetings and yet the tide had not turned. Movies and television added to this struggle by portraying the extremes of working women, ranging from hostile, cold tyrants to fun-loving playmates of exploitation. The balanced perception of faithful, hard-working women who sought to help clients, create businesses, and redistribute market share had somehow not made the news or impacted the media!

As I sat there, I realized that if women are to change the landscape of the business realm, we must dismantle incorrect perceptions regarding the "acceptable role" of women, first in our own minds, then in the minds of the male business fraternity. Women can embrace their femininity and still succeed personally and professionally. They do not need to decide whether they will be a mom or business owner; it is okay to be both! The traditional definitions of what we can be, or do, and where we can or cannot do them are no longer applicable. We can be ourselves!

While I have shared this one instance with you, this book is not based on just one experience. There have been many. Nor is this book the result of a specific moment where I knew I had to write to women. Rather, it is birthed from countless times of taking a deep breath and crossing over "the line" into male-dominated meetings and assuring myself that I had a right to be there. This book is not experimental or theoretical, but rather experiential and real.

Socialization is a powerful force. Cultures have used shame and disapproval to keep individuals boxed into generally approved roles, and thereby they have perpetuated themselves for centuries. But at what cost? Enormous cost! For this socialization has robbed every culture of the passionate, creative contributions of millions of individuals, male and female alike.

Of course, in this book we are focusing on women, for their role has been suppressed for centuries. Had it not been the urgent need for women to take on the jobs of men who were serving overseas in World War II, the role of women might still be relegated to the home. But all of those capable female workers forever dispelled the notion that they could not do the work or provide the leadership of men.

Just as the African-Americans of that era used their demonstrated performance to break out of the bondage of discrimination and secure full rights through the civil rights movement, so also have women been breaking through similar barriers. The difference is that women must first conquer the wrong thoughts that have been imprinted on them through socialization. That breakthrough happens on an individual basis and over time, challenging and neutralizing one wrong belief after another. As the inner victory is realized, the external triumph will be manifested.

For others to understand and accept the value and gift of our womanhood, we must first accept ourselves, clarify our callings, and become comfortable in our own skins. We must give ourselves permission to come out of hiding.

Women cannot expect that men will be the first to discard the incorrect perceptions about the role of women and invite them into "their" world. We must be the first to step forward and reject the limiting perceptions of ourselves and our womanhood. These limiting perceptions have become incorrectly entrenched in our minds and in the workplace as realities.

For others to understand and accept the value and gift of our womanhood, we must first accept ourselves, clarify our callings, and become comfortable in our own skins. We must give ourselves permission to come out of hiding and embrace our true identity. For it is only when we choose to step out of culturally restraining roles, redefine our true character, and in essence, discover our true DNA, that we can *Keep the Curls* and experience success personally and professionally!

Realize and Discover NOW the Hidden CEO DNA Codes within You!

As I share my story, my hope is to show you that within you, within every woman, can be found the CEO (Chief Executive Officer) DNA codes of administration, operations, sales/marketing, and finance. While the revelation that all women carry these codes within them is liberating, and can birth generational culture change, it finds resistance not only from the opposite gender, but from within the internal ranks of women as well! Daring to defy the traditional perceptions of a woman's "position" can seem rebellious, unsubmissive, and even "unladylike." But, when we, as women, realize that the initial definitions were drawn incorrectly, we can experience the freedom to break those confining rules. When we reject the incorrect programming received as children, we can celebrate our femininity and still have significant and lasting impact in every sphere we enter.

I hope this book will encourage you and the women in your life to see the unique creation that all of us are. High heels cannot only keep up with, but even go beyond the oxfords! Women, keep your curls and take the place you were created to occupy personally and professionally. Release the hidden CEO Codes within you. Become all you were created to be!

Section I:

Understanding
the CEO DNA Codes

We Are a Generation of Game Changers!

The fun part of being a woman is that we were born this way! That is a simple concept, but one we often relinquish to gain approval. We CAN *Keep the Curls* and still experience success, both personally and professionally. The CEO codes that make us unique and help set us apart have already been instilled within us. We don't have to wear a suit, act out a role, or fit into a mold to earn the right to play in the game of life! **We are the generation of game changers.** Our awakening to the presence of these CEO DNA codes will dismantle the need for acceptance into the "Boys Club." Being our feminine selves, in every regard, will change our quality of life and, as an added benefit, create a level playing field for our daughters for generations to come!

Chapter 1

Women and
the Hidden CEO Within

I stood at the bay window in the kitchen, nervously shifting my weight back and forth as my dad's car sped down our driveway. I knew that we only had two hours to begin (and end) my transformation. That's not much time to change a "stay-at-home" mom into a professional business-woman with the poise and confidence needed to stand her ground in the workplace. There were business suits to buy, shoes to try on, and of course, the ever-popular makeover that would tame my tangled curls into submission.

I felt a blast of cold air as he rushed into my kitchen and asked if I was ready to go. I bent down to my three-year-old daughter, making sure her coat was zippered, hoisted her to my hip, grabbed my purse and headed towards his car. I was leaving as a frazzled home-loving, kid-hugging mom and would return as a professionally-manicured performer ready to enter the business world on Monday morning.

Our first stop was a chain of clothing stores. We hurriedly perused the racks, looking for blue or black suits—not too baggy but not too tight—we didn't want anything that would draw attention to my gender. I lugged several suits back to the dressing room, one finger turning blue from the weight of the hangers and the other turning red from the questioning tug of my three-year-old as she repeatedly asked, "Mum, where you goin'?"

I didn't know how to explain all this to my three-year-old. She only knew me as her Play Dough playmate and the world's best cookie maker. She didn't know that there was a whole other world out there that some mommies must learn to play in and hopefully survive. There are invisible rules and guidelines that are like hidden land mines. You don't know when you've stepped on one by saying or doing something wrong until it's too late and the bomb goes off! Casualties are widespread among women in the workplace; their spirits are killed through internal wounding, as their identities bleed out. It's a dangerous world for the uninformed, naïve woman.

**I was losing a part of me, all in an effort
to be a part of them—the ever-elusive, verbally
unspoken "Boys Club."**

I sat her on the dressing room stool as I tried one suit after another, but nothing fit or looked right. I just couldn't find *me*. We left empty-handed and headed to the hair salon in a last-ditch attempt to fit into my new world. I unwound my daughter from my neck and smiled at her as I headed to the chair. "She needs professional. She needs to be taken seriously. She needs to get rid of the curls," were the instructions from my well-meaning dad, who was trying to position me to succeed.

I knew it was true. I had to be taken seriously. I had to prove I could think, articulate, and add value to my new company. So I sat watching one curl of femininity after another slowly unwind and drop to the floor. Years of memories of little fingers soothing themselves to sleep while they played with mommy's hair came to an end as I watched the stylist stand on the piles that now littered the ground. Tears slipped from my eyes as I knew I was losing more than just curls. I was losing a part of me, all in an effort to be a part of them—the ever-elusive, verbally unspoken "Boys Club."

Although you may not have experienced this exact scenario, as women we know there has been an invisible set of guidelines in the business realm. If we want to play in the Boys Club, we must run faster, be stronger, and last longer. There is no room for feelings, emotions, sick children, family problems, or any type of weakness. We have been trained to blend in and mold ourselves into the roles presented to us. There is little room for variation, and if attempted, judgment swiftly pronounced and a sentence of exclusion executed.

While this may have been an acceptable practice in the past, we can no longer continue down this path. It is time for women to rise and embrace the innate qualities and capabilities that have been placed within them. There are CEO DNA codes that have been impregnated, in seed form, within each of us through an intentional design created and sealed forever at the time of our conception. It is critical that we awaken and cultivate these codes. We hold the strategic component that has been lacking in our families, business realms, communities, and culture.

I am not implying that men are not needed, but rather that we, as women, must not try to step into the role created for them. Instead, we must embrace the strength of womanhood and the impact that a woman, a mother, and a CEO can have in her various spheres of influence. These areas include family, business, education, government, media, religion, arts, and entertainment. As we recognize and become intentional regarding our femininity, we can move in collaborative power with men who are confident in their callings, and together create a lasting and generational legacy!

Keep the Curls!

We have been so indoctrinated with what the world feels is "professional" that we have traded our life-giving, atmosphere-changing, sphere-impacting heritage for polished dress-up clothes that we wear to define us in the workplace. Let's shatter the perception that we must conform to that which is culturally or religiously acceptable. Instead, let us embrace and breathe life into the full capacity of who we are as women!

Let us embrace and breathe life into the full capacity of who we are as women!

The fun part of being a woman is that we were born this way! That is a simple concept, but one we often relinquish to gain approval. We CAN *Keep the Curls* and still experience success, both personally and professionally. The CEO codes that make us unique and help set us apart have already been instilled within us. We don't have to wear a suit, act out a role, or fit into a mold to earn the right to play in the game of life! **We are the generation of game changers.** Our awakening to the presence of these CEO DNA codes will dismantle the need for acceptance into the "Boys Club." Being our feminine selves, in every regard, will change our quality of life and, as an added benefit, create a level playing field for our daughters for generations to come!

The freedom now exists to break the crippling roles displayed through our culture and paraded on television and full-length movies. The celebrated media images of women casting themselves as male "wannabes" in order to be successful will ultimately be revealed as the sham it has always been. No longer will a woman's intellect be ridiculed as a rarity or accepted only when cloaked by a man's persona. **The reality is that we are designed to be successful as women. All we need to do is to cultivate that which is already within us!**

The first battle to be won is within our minds. There must be an internal shifting of perception of our worth as women in order for us to embrace our CEO DNA Codes. This shifting will provide us with the unique insight and capabilities to oversee and impact homes, businesses, communities, and entire cultures. We cannot implement change that we have not first accepted ourselves!

Personal Buy-In

When my children were younger, I would take them clothes shopping for school. I would set a budget and let them know the amount of money they had to work with. They would scour the newspaper looking for sales and create a game plan of attack. They plotted which store we needed to visit and what they would purchase. There usually came a time during our shopping spree where they found an unexpected item that they "couldn't live without!" Yet, it often was outside the budget. At that point, they had a decision to make. They could either return the item to the rack and walk away empty-handed, or they could initiate personal buy-in by using their own resources to purchase the outfit. When I saw that they were willing to put their own money on the line, I knew the outfit had become a non-negotiable item and was worth the additional expense.

As women, we must come to a place of personal buy-in. We can't expect others to pay the price for our success.

They can point the way, but we must take responsibility for our own growth. During the course of this book, you will receive insight designed to help you identify the CEO DNA Codes within you. Through practical real life examples, you will see illustrations that can be applied to you as a woman, a mother, wife, employee, or business owner. Implementing these truths can increase your effectiveness as you navigate through life, family, and the business realm.

Although some CEO DNA codes are initially more recognizable to you than others, all of them are ingrained in each of us and require activation. I encourage you to invest in yourself and exert the effort and time required to cultivate these skill sets. If we allow ourselves, each of us will experience a defining moment where we understand the personal cost involved and decide that we "can't live without it." Only then can we embrace the deeper reality of who we are and pay the price for a new level of freedom. If we fail to do so, we will put this revelation back on the rack and return to our lives of quiet desperation, lives controlled by the hindering mindsets of the past. *Which option will you choose?*

We Have the Codes!

I had a garage sale at which I displayed a wide array of jewelry that I didn't want anymore. On some pieces I couldn't find the second earring, for others the clasp wasn't working, others were just tarnished. Honestly, I saw them as just plain useless. The sale started and right away a gentleman walked in and headed straight for my jewelry carton. He began sifting through and picking up pieces, holding them to the light and weighing them in his hand.

As I watched his scrutiny, I began to wonder if I had been too hasty in my decision to discard those pieces. Perhaps there was value that I wasn't seeing. I just saw them as old, used-up, lackluster clutter that needed to be traded for whatever coin I could receive in return. But this man saw value; he had plans and hopes for those pieces. He had the vision to look past the surface to the value within. As women, we must embrace that same ability. We must realize that women are not pieces of costume jewelry of insignificant value; we are priceless human beings birthed with CEO DNA. We must stop throwing ourselves into the garage sale heap. Many times we see ourselves as too old, too broken, or not good enough, and we discount ourselves. We need to pick ourselves up out of the box that we have put ourselves in, blow off the dust of lies, and begin to see ourselves as the Keeper of the Codes!

We must realize that women are not pieces of costume jewelry of insignificant value; we are priceless human beings birthed with CEO DNA.

Once we have recognized our value, we can cultivate these codes through character enhancers. These enhancers include being trustworthy, profitable, hardworking, generous, confident, skillful, respectful, kind, and wise. We can occupy the positions of administrators, managers, teachers, nurturers, financial planners, and creators of legacy. All of this potential placed inside us is begging to be recognized, cultivated, and released into our spheres of influence. Will you reevaluate your value and cultivate its potential? Will you take that step? Will you start to do that now?

CEO—Chief Executive Officer

My daughter came home from a conference the other day so excited. She had participated in a lecture given by the first woman CEO of that organization. She was in awe! She raved about how this woman spoke, how she took charge, and how much was learned during that short conference. This woman had motivated her to become a CEO someday.

I had to remind her, her someday is now! Ladies, we have the seeds to be a CEO and it's not years from now, but today! We are Chief Executives Officers of our personal lives, our families, our institutions, and our business environment.

Ladies, we have the seeds to be a CEO and it's not years from now, but today!

A CEO is just a fancy title indicating the person who is the "sphere influencer" and "vision caster" of an organization. This person must be able to oversee administration, operations, sales/marketing, and finance. A CEO will determine the culture of the environment and set the parameters regarding the success and well-being of a company.

Now before you disqualify yourself by thinking this doesn't apply to you, think about this: Have you heard the phrase, "If Mama ain't happy, ain't nobody happy?" Who is setting the atmosphere in that environment? If you don't think you already have serious influence, think again! You surely have it, but the key is to be aware of it, so you can be more intentional about the things you do and how you do them.

How about the famous *Honey Do List*? Ever made one of those? Then welcome to Administration 101! You already have the goods, just increase your awareness! Permit me to ask you, "When little Bobby punches sister Susie and things get out of line at home, who is called in?" Wouldn't that be you, the Director of Operations? One more question,

"How are your coupon-cutting activities influencing your cash flow results?" That is finance in motion! You are more capable than you have allowed yourself to acknowledge. But you can change that, starting now! As you can see, you are a functioning CEO in administration, operations, sales/marketing, and finance. As the head of these departments, you need to be knowledgeable regarding your impact.

I remember when I was still at home raising my children. At the end of each day, I would listen for the sound of my husband coming home. He owns a trucking business and at that time, he was one of the drivers. Our road had an S-turn in it, and you could hear him downshifting as he came around the corner. If you were paying attention, you could hear him long before you could ever see him. Many times when I was playing with the kids on the floor, I would hear his truck in the distance and knew he would be home soon.

I had a split-second decision to make. Was I going to promote my husband and celebrate his return? Or, would I continue to play on the floor and make his entrance a non-event in our daily routine?

I chose to celebrate! I would whisk the kids up into my arms and excitedly declare, "I hear Daddy coming! I hear Daddy coming!"

We would run to the window and I would balance them on the windowsill as they pressed their little noses onto the glass, trying to see him. At the first glimpse of his truck, their chubby little hands would begin to wave and bang on the windows in excitement! They would look back at me and I would smile and help them clap their hands, showing them my excitement for his arrival. Every day we would repeat this, and every day they learned to be excited that "Da-Da" was home!

You can call this overdramatic and silly, or good parenting, or whatever you would like to call it, but regardless, I was making a sales decision. I was the Director of Sales/ Marketing in my personal life, my home, and my business. I had determined that I would provide whatever information and supporting documentation that was needed for my children to understand that I was in love with their father, I enjoyed him, and I looked forward to seeing him every day. I wanted them to know that I felt he was trustworthy and a critical part of our lives. Jumping to the window may seem dramatic, but it closed the sale! Today, all my children are grown and on their own. Each one of them loves, respects, and enjoys a relationship with their father.

**I was making a sales decision.
I was the Director of Sales/Marketing in
my personal life, my home, and my business.**

The departments of administration, operations, sales/ marketing, and finance are innate abilities created within women. The seeds of our potential have been embedded in us, from the time of our conception. We innately administrate, operate, conduct financial transactions, market, and sell on a daily basis. Some women have recognized these characteristics within and have begun to sharpen their skill sets. Others are just now waking up to the realization that the seeds have been there all along. No matter which category you identify with, we are all women CEOs who impact the culture around us through our lives, businesses, and families.

So, strap on your high heels, ladies. It is time to discover all that you have to offer. It is time to embrace the person you really are and the CEO DNA Codes within you!

Ask Yourself...

- Are you ready to accept a new perception regarding the true value of a woman in the home, business realm, community, and culture?
- List areas where you have traded your femininity in an attempt to enter the "Boys Club."
- What areas of your womanhood have you told to be quiet and have subsequently suppressed?
- Are you willing to recognize and participate in the "buy-in" regarding the CEO within you?
- What innate things do you naturally do that reveal the seeds of the CEO DNA codes within?
- When others try to discount you, how have you responded, and how will that now change?
- Who are you trying to please with your life? Are you willing to risk doing greater things?
- Are you willing to think and color outside the lines of what a woman is "supposed" to be?
- List three areas where you will begin to cultivate your femininity.

Fullness of Life!

Must a woman give up her individual destiny as part of a culturally accepted (and expected) rite of passage as she moves from womanhood to motherhood to business leader? Never! That is a concept that is both life inhibiting and counterproductive; one which must be challenged whenever and wherever it surfaces. Life is not about an "either/or" situation, rather, it is a "fullness of life" issue. Each season of life is a transition, where we move upward, going to greater and greater levels of effectiveness and fulfillment.

Chapter 2

Identity Crisis Solved!

As a mother, some of my favorite times were snuggling up with my children and watching a good movie. One of their favorite flicks was *The Ugly Dachshund*—the story of a couple who decided to raise a family of puppies. The husband wanted a strong, ferocious puppy that he could raise into a dominating, powerful alpha male. On the other hand, the wife wanted only females—lap dogs that she could dress up and display. As they searched for the perfect compromise, the husband found a beautiful Great Dane and the wife found four little female dachshunds. The couple had selected two breeds from the opposite ends of the spectrum!

As the story unfolded, each "parent" worked with their charges to prove they had purchased the superior breed. The husband worked diligently, training and instilling "manly" mannerisms into his dog. Yet, no matter how much training and attention was given, this beautiful Great Dane would watch the four other puppies and mimic all their "feminine" behaviors. He would crawl around on his belly, trying to be the same height as the little dachshunds; he would attempt to jump onto the lap of the wife, crawl under the couch or small tables just like the dachshunds, and otherwise behave like one of them. Of course, regardless of how hard he tried, he never succeeded! He could never do anything exactly like the dachshunds. He was always too big and too clumsy to be accepted as one of them. In fact, the more he tried to fit in, the more problems he created, and the more determined the wife became to get rid of him.

Months of training and retraining were spent on the Great Dane to help him understand that he couldn't be like the dachshunds. Over and over again he was told that no matter how hard he tried, he would never be able to be like them. He had to accept the fact that in spite of his greatest efforts and all professional training, he would never be able to do what came naturally, and simply, to the dachshunds.

The owners realized that focusing on changing the behavior of the Great Dane was not the answer. His conduct was not the real issue; the real problem was the belief system within the Great Dane. Because he had been around the dachshunds for his entire life and had always tried to mimic them, he had come to believe that he was a dachshund.

One day his owners placed him with a group of Great Danes. Immediately he began to see himself in a different light. He noticed how they walked, stood, barked, and played. He watched how they carried themselves and admired the nobility of their posture. Suddenly, his ears perked up, his legs stretched out, and he stopped groveling on the ground and displaying other dachshund behaviors. He stopped trying to be something he was never created to be once he discovered who he really was.

From that day forward, he walked differently, interacted with his owners differently, and, most importantly, he was no longer influenced by the behaviors of the dachshunds. He finally understood that while he had grown up with the dachshunds, he wasn't one of them. He didn't need to struggle to be one. He could stand tall and be the Great Dane he was destined to be, because he finally knew who he was!

Many women are like the Great Dane in the story. They have been born into an environment in which they have altered their natural tendencies and skill sets to mimic those around them. Even though every aspect of their being screams out that they are not a dachshund, they continue to crawl with their belly to the ground, trying to fit in. They are confused when the actions of others are accepted, and sometimes even promoted, and yet when they attempt to perform the very same actions, they don't get the same results. They try harder, work longer, and sacrifice more in their attempt for validation regarding their true identity. These uninformed and unaware women are trying to play by the cultural or religious rule book. They allow culture to require them to quietly blend into their surroundings and succumb to the expectations of others.

These uninformed and unaware women are trying to play by the cultural or religious rule book. They allow culture to require them to quietly blend into their surroundings and succumb to the expectations of others.

The day of awakening must come in which women begin to celebrate the difference between men and women. They must embrace the CEO DNA skill sets instilled within them, as wives, mothers, sisters, and as businesswomen outside the home.

With boldness and joy, women must dare to believe that we were created to be different in all respects, and that these differences are to be celebrated and uniquely developed—not subjugated. This realization must be birthed, nurtured, and grown from within ourselves before we can expect others to see us differently and be willing to accept the new definition of our roles. No amount of external training can bring true freedom and acceptance until an internal shift within oneself has transpired.

As we seek to discover ourselves, we must understand that womanhood is not about labeling, creating a definition, or providing an excuse. We are not seeking to create a revolution in the sense of rebelliously throwing off our femininity and responsibilities. Women are not about "reinventing" themselves or creating a "movement." Rather, women must be given permission to understand themselves so that in turn, they might be understood by others. It is time for us to see ourselves as gifts: gifts to ourselves, to our families, to the workplace, and to future generations. It is the season for awakening, embracing, and understanding the uniqueness that infuses our female DNA.

It is the season for awakening, embracing, and understanding the uniqueness that infuses our female DNA.

As we arise and shake off false expectations and cultural cloning, we can see that the CEO skill sets deposited in seed form within women, when activated, can change the world. Culture cries for women to have equality with men. However, earning the same as a man doing the same job doesn't impart to a woman anything more than a paycheck; it does not validate her true identity. Equality is more than financial recognition; it extends to a deeper more influential level. It is the ability to walk into a room and have equal standing regarding the impact and influence of your words and decisions. It is an aura of openness and competence that causes the thought processes and insights of women to be sought, embraced, and valued. The quote, "The hand that rocks the cradle rules the world," is just a small glimpse of the vast influence and authority that women can carry not only within the home, but within the community and business realm as well.

The Emotional Process within Your Identity

As you embrace the realization that you are designed to function in the full capacity of your feminine giftings, you may experience backlash. Let me explain.

As we know, every individual has specific strengths and weaknesses within their personalities, whether male or female. These are not necessarily gender-based, but rather they are linked to the personality profiles within an individual. Studies have shown that learning the framework of your personality tendencies can help provide you with an overview as to why you perform or react in a specific way regarding situations. You will notice that when your strengths are pushed beyond their limits, they actually become weaknesses that stress out and ultimately derail your attempts to progress forward. This is an important concept to understand. For many women, when their sensitivity and insight into the feelings and mood of a situation are pushed to an extreme, they react emotionally. This lack of discipline and misunderstanding on how to effectively use this insight has earned women the "prestigious" label of being "overly emotional."

Emotions are not wrong; in fact, emotions are a gateway that allows us to embrace life. In spite of what you may have heard, or have been trained regarding your emotions, they are not evil and are intended to be used for good. Yet, like any strength not kept under control, emotions can have undesirable repercussions. They can become a weakness and cause damage to ourselves and others. Excessive emotionalism among women has been universally criticized by our culture, resulting in a generally negative reflection on us all. This one area has helped to support the myth that the capabilities of a woman are of questionable value In fact, the concept of a woman "being emotional" has evolved into an accepted expectation that has enabled women to be undisciplined in that regard. This provides men with the basis to prevent women from holding positions of influence.

Emotional intelligence among women must increase. It is not the shutting down or denying of our emotions. Rather, women need to develop both the awareness of and the ability to control their thoughts and related emotive reactions instead of being controlled by them.

Emotional intelligence is not yet a common topic within books written on self-development or self-improvement. Yet, we must mature in our emotions just like we mature intellectually and physically. We must also grow in our understanding and capability to effectively communicate both our thoughts and emotions to ourselves and others in reasonable but effective ways.

Emotional intelligence[1] deals with the ability to understand your emotions so that you can truly understand what is "moving," or going on behind the scenes, in a given situ-

---

[1] Since 1990, Peter Salovey and John D. Mayer have been the leading researchers on emotional intelligence. In their influential article, "Emotional Intelligence," they defined emotional intelligence as, "the subset of social intelligence that involves the ability to monitor one's own and others' feelings and emotions, to discriminate among them, and to use this information to guide one's thinking and actions" (1990).

Salovey and Mayer proposed a model that identified four different factors of emotional intelligence: the perception of emotion, the ability reason using emotions, the ability to understand emotion, and the ability to manage emotions.

http://psychology.about.com/od/personalitydevelopment/a/emotionalintell.htm

ation or in the lives surrounding you. It provides the ability to acknowledge and honor one's feelings regarding a matter without violating the boundaries and perceptions of others! It is not about assessing a situation as to who is right or wrong, but rather the ability to discern what is happening in the emotional realm without being held captive to it.

We must also grow in our understanding and capability to effectively communicate both our thoughts and emotions to ourselves and others in reasonable but effective ways.

Unchallenged emotions create self-imposed prisons in which thoughts, voices, and situations reinforce the distorted perceptions and beliefs. The food provided to those inmates always includes a healthy serving of justification. Everything they believe must be justified. If a woman believes that she does not have the skill set and the ability to grow the DNA seeds that have been planted within her since birth, then she will spend her years justifying this belief. Over time a self-image will be developed that reinforces that distorted thinking.

We search after and attract those who will validate these feelings and view those people as friends, even if they are reinforcing wrong thoughts and perceptions. How many women continue to stay with men who abuse them or remain in degrading home situations because their belief systems tell them that no one else would love them? Or, they stay in unhealthy work situations because they believe that they do not possess the skill set to get a job somewhere else? In either instance, they believed a lie—hook, line, and sinker, and are drowning in their lack of emotional intelligence. They have let their emotions and culture dictate their belief system—not reality.

We must increase our emotional intelligence and correctly fortify our self-image so that we do not accept the boxes others try to put us in nor fall prey to the boxes we unwittingly create for ourselves.

When you are in the box and closed down to emotional intelligence, you are in a stance of justification; you don't want the situation to change because you want be justified in your feelings. So you sabotage yourself, your family, and the business environment around you to ensure that they line up with the beliefs that you are carrying. In time, those situations may become as you have believed.

It's time to silence the irrational presumptions about yourself and others. Lose the drama, stop reacting to life, and get out of the boxes you or others have created.

Many times women like being in the center of an emotional crisis. They have found their identity in being saved. It's time to silence the irrational presumptions about yourself and others. Lose the drama, stop reacting to life, and get out of the boxes you or others have created. You are woman enough to lead a life without needing a crisis to validate your existence.

Does that mean we don't show emotions of displeasure? Do we stop correcting others and go back to letting people walk all over us? Absolutely not! As CEOs who have the ability to bring order to situations as part of our DNA, we are capable of walking with integrity and releasing wise counsel to those around us. However, correction given by one trapped within the box of justification is seldom received. It is only when one can speak without needing to justify, that true communication can happen.

The Mechanical Processes Impacting Our Identity

We need to move past the point where we are waiting for permission to be granted in order to take action. We have the mandate to come out of hiding, embrace our femininity, and impact our culture. This will require action.

Our first step is to stop defaulting to the lowest common denominator when it comes to our expectations. Too often a woman believes her choices lie only between one option or another.

Must a woman give up her individual destiny as part of a culturally accepted (and expected) rite of passage as she moves from womanhood to motherhood to business leader? Never! That is a concept that is both life inhibiting and counterproductive; one which must be challenged whenever and wherever it surfaces. Life is not about an "either/or" situation, rather, it is a "fullness of life" issue. Each season of life is a transition, where we move upward, going to greater and greater levels of effectiveness and fulfillment.

I have a good friend who maintained a high-paying, highly visible financial position in a Fortune 500 company. She was wise with her resources and had begun to amass significant wealth. My friend was in her late thirties when she met her husband, and within two years, she was expecting a child. As you can imagine, she was extremely excited but nervous. This was a new chapter in her life that would require a new alignment of priorities and finances. After much consideration, she decided that she would resign from her current position and take the next five years to stay at home with her child. She could live off her investments, and if finances grew tight, she would explore avenues for generating income.

As we sat together and discussed this option, she explained that she would not accept the "deactivation" of her business skill set as a viable option for her future. She was a brilliant woman capable of great intellectual decisions and financial management. She believed that despite the mantra, "you can't have your cake and eat it too," that she indeed would not only have her cake, but she would get extra icing as well!

So we strategized; we developed a plan. She would begin to take the classes necessary to pursue an area of expertise that she had always wanted to explore: *financial coaching for women in transition.* She would customize a program that would help high-powered executives take their CEO DNA Codes and multiply them into places of life expansion and personal development. Women would have the coaching they needed to be moms, business owners, and employees of influence. They would have the support they needed to effectively transition from CEO of organizations to CEO of their own lives and homes as well.

She defied the concept of expecting new situations to cause defaults in other areas of her life. Changing seasons is not a trade-off; it's an enlargement! No longer should we expect to step backwards, but rather we must awaken to the fact that every day and every experience prepares and propels us forward into a deeper revelation and experience of our inner CEO codes!

This advancement will not happen just because we wish it, think it, or even because we are improving our emotional intelligence skill set. It is a built-in combination with internal preparation and requires outward effort and manifestation. It is the boldness to push forward and take hold of the concrete steps needed to equip ourselves for destiny activation. If my friend had not studied to prepare and equip herself, if she had not taken the courses and the certifications needed, then she would not have been stretched to sharpen the CEO skills within and would have disqualified herself from advancement.

Too often, we disqualify ourselves as a result of fear, ignorance, doubt, or a lack of confidence. We must be bold and train ourselves in the areas of expertise available to us. We cannot be under the disillusionment that it will be an easy and bloodless battle. I have yet to meet a seasoned, accomplished woman warrior without scars! Yet, take comfort in the fact that while we step forward and fight, our skills will sharpen in the battle and our perseverance will lead us to victory!

The success of effectively implementing the mechanical process of our CEO DNA Codes is dependent upon the internal foundation. This foundation is created through understanding and establishing emotional intelligence. The tedious and hidden work of dismantling incorrect perceptions and reconstructing a healthy belief system is done internally but creates the platform for the visible actions. Outward actions are dictated by inward directions. Therefore it is imperative that the inner compass be correctly aligned.

Individuals will often come into my financial planning office and ask me what mechanical processes they need to implement in order to experience great wealth. Despite their age or gender, my answer is always the same, "You must become wealthy in your mind, long before it ever shows up in your checking account." The thought processes and belief system must be in alignment and firmly rooted in wisdom, knowledge, and understanding. Once the correct beliefs are in place, then the emotional processes of finances must be addressed. Does the discussion of finances pull the strings of reaction and drive you to respond? Or have you mastered your emotions so that the puppet has finally become the puppeteer?

Your beliefs dictate who you become. What you believe, you think, and then you speak, which produces action. And for every action, there is a reaction. This reaction then validates and justifies your thinking, and so the cycle continues. You speak out of perceptional understanding, which causes actions of alignment, which produce results. These results are dependent upon the belief. Change the belief; change the result.

So, how does this apply to the lost identity of women? Here are just a few of the lies we have believed:

- *Women are inferior beings whose primary purpose is to serve their husbands and families.*
- *Women were not created to assume leadership roles in the workplace.*
- *Women are weak and can easily be swayed.*
- *Women should not work outside the home.*
- *Women are too emotional to be in positions of influence.*

These are just a few of the ingrained lies that have been accepted as truths within our culture. They have become beliefs, producing verbal acceptance, reinforced by the mechanical processes of living the lie. To question them has seemed rebellious, disrespectful, and borderline iconic Jezebel in nature. Yet, nothing could be further from the truth. It is not rebellion to embrace our identity as equipped women who are capable and called for womanhood, motherhood, and the business realm. Rather, it is rebellion to know that you have the seeds of the CEO DNA Codes within you and yet let them remain dormant until they die!

So let's take the next few chapters and explore these principles, their purposes, and how they intertwine and support each other. Let's unlock the CEO code that is within YOU as a woman! This code will provide the systems and structures for resources to flow abundantly, be stewarded effectively, invested wisely, and multiplied for the future.

There are four key areas that need to be addressed. Each one of them is currently within the DNA structure of women. At the core of the CEO DNA Codes are:

- Administration
- Operations
- Sales/Marketing
- Finance

Each one of these codes has been ingrained within women so successfully that many are unaware that they own these codes. We must grab hold of our inner spiritual, emotional, and mental processes of advancement, stretch our legs, strap on our heels, and stride forward!

Ask Yourself...

1. What is your definition of emotional intelligence?
2. Since unchallenged emotions create self-imposed prisons, what areas do you need to begin to challenge in order to create new thought patterns?
3. Identify three areas where you have defaulted to the lowest common denominator and traded one pathway of passion for another.
4. Your beliefs help dictate what you become. Are you pleased with the direction you are headed? If not, what thought processes can you change?

You Innately Administrate...

How many women have written down a chore list for your children or your husband? We affectionately call this the "Honey Do List," although I am sure they have other names for it! In the marketplace, those who own businesses have charts and systems that we put into place to create a pattern for office life to continue to flow smoothly. We call it being organized, on track or, if pushed to an extreme, micromanaging. Yet, despite what it is called, in the core form, it is administration.

Chapter 3

CEO Code of Administration: The "List"

It was another crowded Sunday at the local eatery. I scanned the room looking hopefully for some place we could eat, talk, and still be heard. Outside tables beckoned, but in this heat, I was not interested in their offer! A little early, I moved to the side, leaned against the wall, and began the humorous game of people watching! Time passed quickly and soon I saw her rushing across the parking lot, frantically checking her watch. She dashed in through the double doors, and with a quick swipe at her brow, she began the process of locating me. I caught her eye and we headed towards the food!

Settling at our table, the conversation ran along the surface as we talked weather, family, and weekend activities. As our forks clicked the empty salad bowls, our conversation turned to the matter at hand. We were here to birth a business.

"So, tell me," I asked, "What are your goals and where exactly do you see your business going?"

I didn't really expect her to have an answer; I knew this process of interrogation would be new to her. While it would be uncomfortable, it was a much-needed rite of passage! I had met too many women who had skipped this step and jumped straight into opening a business, only to have it fail within a year. Business and personal bankruptcy had claimed enough victims; I was not interested in letting it have one more.

As she stammered through a vague overview of the concept, I began the process of gingerly applying pressure.

"I will need a list of goals you want to achieve and the time frame in which you believe they should be completed. In addition, I am interested in knowing if this business is the end result, or are you building it for credibility so you can platform off into other ventures?"

"Also, what are your financial expectations?"

"Are you looking for mentoring or a business partner?"

"What are your strengths and weaknesses, and where do you believe you are most vulnerable?"

The questions came in rapid procession. Each question was posed with the intent to discover the depth of her understanding and the strength of her conviction. She was young, but there was no mistaking that the seeds of entrepreneurship were taking root within her. With mentoring, some solid administrative guidance, a dedication to implement the plan, and foresight in marketing, this young woman could be a prosperous force to be reckoned with in just a few short years!

As I began to strategically piece together her answer, I began the process of planning called "administration." This would be her lifeline, and if used effectively, could be reproducible for additional businesses to come.

While administration is not necessarily difficult, it does require thought and time. It is essential in every sphere of life and is something women do every day, although many don't realize it. Administration is creating an intentional plan for the purpose of positioning for a desired outcome.

The ongoing "to do" lists must effectively execute the intentional plan. Administration provides a pathway to meet the end need or to display a service that we want to provide. It is a behind-the-scenes evaluation, combined with an upfront plan of implementation. We must have administration in order for a person, family, or business to reach the next level. It is your game plan of attack. It shows the beginning and the end and all the required steps in between! When life gets hard and the waves get high, this is the compass that keeps emotion from running you aground.

Administration is creating an intentional plan for the purpose of positioning for a desired outcome.

Many people dream about doing what they love. They want to focus on just that area and think everything will work out fine. Yet life on all levels requires an intentional plan. These plans range from understanding the steps required in raising and instilling character within a child, to the wisdom and insight needed for the development and DNA structure of a business. We must realize that passion or love for a specific goal is never enough. There must be an intentional plan to get there!

I remember a doctor who visited my financial planning office; he was extremely frustrated. He told me how he had spent years and hundreds of thousands of dollars learning how to help people. He loved the medical field and enjoyed the ability to sit down with his patients, diagnose the problem, and provide them with a solution. Yet his biggest complaint was that despite all the medical training he received, there had been no administrative business training. In all the years he had attended college, nothing had prepared him to run a successful business.

Now a discouraged physician sat before me contemplating bankruptcy. He couldn't comprehend how he could be so passionate and committed to help others and yet still have it all fall apart. His bills weren't paid and there was little to no income left to take care of his own family. In essence, his practice was falling apart.

This doctor is like many business owners and parents; they believe that one's passion and love for a child, an occupation, or a business is enough to make it grow. Like newlyweds, they have stars in their eyes declaring that their love is enough and that they don't need money or a plan. They fantasize that they will succeed and live happily ever after! This may sound facetious, but I am sure many of us have encountered these diehard romantics. And yet, just like our doctor, they end up near bankruptcy with their families in shambles, confused and wondering how it all fell apart. Why weren't we able to build a lasting marriage, a strong family, a successful business, or enduring legacy? Why wasn't "love" enough?

The encouraging part is that in the end, when structured properly, love can be enough! There is nothing more appealing than entering a loving, nurturing home or going to a place of business where the staff loves what they do. They go the extra mile, they care, they are happy, and the client/patient is provided exceptional service. But here is the caveat. In order for parents to raise emotionally healthy and well-balanced children, and in order for business owners to create an environment where they and their employees love to work, and they, as the owners, are able to focus solely upon what they love to do, there must be an understanding of the principles and purposes of administration. There must also be an understanding of how administration affects a home and the operation of a business.

You've Already Got This!

How many women have written down a chore list for your children or your husband? We affectionately call this the "Honey Do List," although I am sure they have other names for it! In the marketplace, those who own businesses have charts and systems that we put into place to create a pattern for office life to continue to flow smoothly. It's the "to do" list. We call it being organized and on track or, if pushed to an extreme, micromanaging. Yet, despite what it is called, in the core form, it is administration.

Women have the innate ability to administer on several levels. As mothers, we oversee the schedules and activities of our children. We create systems and schedules to make sure everyone arrives at the proper place at the right time. Women establish parameters of what can and cannot be done, along with the rules and systems of what we will allow. As we administrate, we are responsible and have been given the authority to mold and guide the next generation as they mature into our living legacy.

What we must realize is that this skill set of administration empowers women with the ability to assess a situation, prioritize the needs and tasks that require attention, and then create a plan of order that will allow the home, business, or legacy of future generations to be positioned to thrive. Without it, individuals, families, businesses, and the youth of tomorrow are at the whims of emotions, and are at the mercy of those with the power to implement yet lack the knowledge of know-how.

Administration Creates Practical Steps for Getting Here to There

One of the responsibilities of a CEO is the ability to administrate. It is the skill of understanding the vision and putting practical steps in place for implementation. In essence, administration is the process of bringing the vision to life and charting the path for growth.

Administration becomes the glue, personally and professionally, that ensures proper positioning in all realms of life.

The formal definition includes "the performance of executive duties" and "management and leadership." The practical, down-to-earth application of this definition is the desire within an individual to see where one needs to go and the ability to uncover the steps required for arriving there! When we administrate, we execute the ability to oversee and create the proper flow of responsibility needed to strengthen the vision and create legacy. Administration becomes the glue, personally and professionally, that ensures proper positioning in all realms of life.

I come from a family of twelve. My mother had discovered and polished her CEO DNA Codes of administration; she understood and was intentional in using her ability! Every day when we came home from school, there was a pattern in place. First we had a snack in the kitchen—usually warm, homemade bread lathered in butter, honey, or peanut butter, depending upon the child! After several huge, thick slices of warm gooeyness, we received our chore list—our "to do" list that would keep our home administration running smoothly. She knew exactly what needed to be accomplished each week in order to effectively run the household.

Since we heated by wood, two of us were sent to the woodpile to either stack wood or bring it in by all the stoves; two were sent to the horse corral to feed, brush, and exercise the horses; two were on lawn duty for our ninety-two acres and had to either mow the lawn or shovel the walks, depending on the season. Last but not least, the remaining children had dish duty, laundry, or housecleaning. Although I admit that I did not appreciate or thank my mom for these administrative skills when I was younger, I see now that her ability to administrate and create order within a household of twelve children was critical! Without it, life would have been disorganized and chaotic.

My mother was an effective administrator. I now see the intentionality of her actions and the way she trained and positioned us so that we could receive the blessings of our efforts in the future. Each one of us, during some part of our working careers, have been told that our work ethic, ability to see projects, and administrate over the steps needed to be taken have played a role in our advancement. We owe that to Mom!

We must disregard the traditional training of having to give up one's dreams or passions to work outside the home in order to have a solid family relationship at home.

Women are gifted to excel at administrating multiple tasks for the various needs of their children and home, in addition to their involvement in business and community. In the past there has been a belief that women could only do one focused role or another: *either they were called to be a mom or a businesswoman, but never both.* This is not true.

As women embedded with the CEO DNA Code of administration, we have the ability to partake in the joys of motherhood and the marketplace. We must disregard the traditional training of having to give up one's dreams or passions to work outside the home in order to have a solid family relationship at home. We carry the ability to administrate and can embrace both worlds. That is part of having life more abundantly!

While administration is a positive ingrained CEO DNA Code within women, many mothers lose themselves within the role of administration and become slaves to the schedules they design. Understanding that they have the authority and the responsibility to create paths of purpose—not schedules of entertainment for their children—can help bring this CEO DNA Code back into proper alignment.

To effectively use the CEO DNA Code of administration, on a personal level, requires taking time to chart a course for one's self. This does not mean abandonment to the family's needs, but rather one first must understand the calling and purpose for her life. You were an individual long before you allowed yourself to enhance your identity in motherhood and the marketplace. Go back and find that woman. What she carries within her will allow you to embrace motherhood and the marketplace without trading your identity!

Schedule Time for Yourself

I have met countless women who can't remember what they like to do, what hobbies they enjoy, or what they would ever do with personal free time. Yet, it is critical that we use administrative skills to carve out personal time; to fit into our schedules time to reflect and refresh our spirits. We need moments that are set aside to nourish our dreams and destinies. It is not uncommon for men to carve out time at the gym or football nights or other activities that allow them "cave time" to be able to process their days and the path they are pursuing. However, the idea of applying the same concept for a woman often causes her to feel selfish for even considering that she might deserve time alone.

Yet, if we are to nurture and expand the effectiveness of the CEO DNA Codes within us, it is mandatory that we quiet our pace and position our spirits for downloads. How else will we know the plans for our personal lives, the lives of our children, our family legacies, and our impact in the marketplace? As women we owe it to ourselves, our families, our businesses, and future generations to love ourselves enough to declare times of refreshing.

Women must be intentional in their pursuit of understanding who they are called to be. It is only when we know ourselves that we in turn can help others.

Women must be intentional in their pursuit of understanding who they are called to be. It is only when we know ourselves that we in turn can help others. When we are running on empty and refuse to refill, we run the risk of "burnout" and the improper use of our CEO DNA Code of administration. Are we running so fast with the lists we have put together that we are creating thoughtless activity, or are we administrating intentional development? We have the skill set within us that allows us to put together the puzzle pieces of life and create a path of purpose!

Our DNA for Administration in the Marketplace

The ability for administration allows us, as employees or business owners, to walk into the marketplace and recognize what needs to be accomplished. Based upon this revelation, we can outline the vision and create systems that cause businesses to prosper!

These procedures can appear evident to all. However, in order for the systems of administration to be received, we must use wisdom. Forcing our decisions and plans upon those around us often brings resistance and resentment. Wisdom provides the ability to take the revelation and together, as a team, implement the strategy.

**A strategy contains a plan of action.
It is not enough to tell those who are following us
that we will succeed; rather, we must provide concrete
systems that can be followed.**

A strategy contains a plan of action. It is not enough to tell those who are following us that we will succeed; rather, we must provide concrete systems that can be followed. The success of your team's journey is correlated to the success of your ability to develop the CEO DNA Code of administration.

Through diligence to implement systems and structures, you will be able to expand your influence in the home, business realm, and your community, and experience a perpetual cycle of growth.

A Challenge

Now is the time to awaken the CEO DNA code of administration that has been sleeping within you. Embrace the truth that you are capable of understanding the vision for your life, the life of your family, and the sphere of your influence in the marketplace. Not only are you equipped with the ability to see the vision, but you also have the wisdom needed to create sustainable impact for today and future generations.

Ask Yourself...

- What administrative skills do you already employ at home and in the workplace that can be translated to other spheres of influence?
- As you plan out your work, do you have goals, objectives, and timelines for things to get done? If not, begin now to write them down.
- What realistic expectations do you have for your home and work environment?
- What new administrative systems need to be put in place so that you can effectively reach your goals within all your spheres of influence?
- Are you intentionally implementing your plan or are you reacting to life?

You Must Be the One to Run with It!

On a personal level, the CEO DNA code of Operations is self-accountability. You set your dream, your expectation, and your hope to where you want to go. You apply the administrative abilities that have already been prewired within you, write your vision down and make it plain so that YOU may run with it. But therein can be found the key—YOU must be the one to run with it.

Chapter 4

CEO Code of Operations:
Getting the Job Done

As they entered my office, all eyes turned towards me. My marketing team had done their job well. They had spread the word and inundated the community with our message: "Crystal Clear Finances could help individuals, couples, and organizations with complex financial planning situations." My administration team had also pulled their weight. They had efficiently answered the numerous phone calls, juggled my calendar, and scheduled the appointments requested. Now it was up to me.

As the clients entered and I turned to shut the door behind them, I saw the hopeful look on my assistant's face as she knew the ball was now completely in my court. Everything we worked for on a daily basis boiled down to the next sixty minutes. If this couple who were now sitting at the conference table were to become my clients, I would need to deliver everything my office had promised, plus a little more.

I took a few moments to explain the procedures of our office and how we conducted business. Then I outlined the services we provided, the products we could use, and a sample of the strategies that could be implemented. Then I moved past the surface explanations and dove a little deeper by explaining that every action was in direct correlation to our company's mission statement: To help individuals of all ages understand the financial realm and take their rightful position within it!

This was more than just a mission statement to our team; it was a way of life. It came from our heartfelt belief that if we are going to have an economic impact in our communities, we need to be able to have financial intelligence and the resources to write the checks to support our vision. We want the authority that comes with being a landowner and the voice of change that comes from proper positioning.

After sharing my heart, I turned to them. Now it was their turn to peel back the layers and begin to share with me their dreams, hopes, and even their fears. I settled back into my chair and as I watched and listened, their story began to unfold. Hesitantly at first, but faster as the comfort grew, they began to move past surface financial expectations and exposed the root issues behind their words. Their story was similar to the hundreds of others that I had heard, and yet it was still uniquely their own. Everyone has a different variation of the same need, and the same cry for financial guidance.

In such moments, individuals reveal the questioning child inside and shift from being a prospect to engaging as a client. My role then becomes very specific and crucial. At that moment of openness and transparency, I am presented with competing choices. Will I become a salesperson and pull out a well-rehearsed line of some product or procedure that they need to buy? Or will I be a conduit of truth and wisdom, regardless of whether or not a sale ever happens? We now step into the critical role of ethical operations that is essential to my office. The people sitting expectantly in front of me need to receive wisdom in regards to their finances. Done correctly, this couple will leave with several concepts to review and ultimately return to implement. This process is repeated several times a day, four days a week, and it is called "operations."

The process of operations is the ability to recognize the interests of an individual, correctly identify the needs, clearly articulate the solution, and then gently encourage a decision. We see operations in every facet of life, including our private home lives. Once again, my mother and my childhood serve as a solid proving ground for this concept. As mentioned previously, my mother was an expert when it came to that function. Perhaps that was due to the fact that I had six brothers and five sisters and we needed some form of organization!

Operations was the process of getting up from the snack and putting into practice the effort needed to complete each chore on that "To Do List."

Operations was the process of getting up from the snack and putting into practice the effort needed to complete each chore on that "To Do List." Sitting in the kitchen eating warm homemade bread and reviewing the list did not create results. No matter how neatly the list was written, regardless of any effort to wish the list away, the only effective means of completing the tasks was to get up and apply the effort needed to get the job done.

I noticed over time that certain chores would be assigned to different individuals within the family. We would have our petty disagreements and come moping to mom that the list was unfair because someone had what we perceived to be a lighter load. The reply was always quick and always the same: "You were not assigned that task because the last few times you were given the opportunity to do the job, it was not done properly. I need to make sure that whoever is responsible for the task will do a quality job."

Being Faithful in the Little Things

At the time, her response never seemed fair. As I grew older, I saw that it was more than appropriate. We know that if we will be faithful in a little, we will be granted more. I have always focused on the "getting more" portion and skimmed past the "applying myself and being faithful in operations" part. But now I understand that when we are given an assignment, we must apply ourselves.

This principle of "being faithful in the little things" applies on all levels. When my office has been faithful to market, administrate, and watch the finances, they are depending upon me to hold up my end of the bargain and to excel in the operations component. As an office, we are a team, and together we win or lose. They all know that when a prospective client has entered my office, it is my turn to be faithful with the "little." It is the moment of true revelation which will uncover if I have been faithful in applying myself and studying so that I might serve these potential clients with excellence. I must ask myself:

- Have I groomed myself to understand others and developed the people skills necessary?
- What about financial knowledge?
- Have I diligently studied and met with product development teams so that I can understand each component?

- If not, then how do I ask for more…and how do I lead a team, knowing I have nothing they should follow?

The Importance of Accountability

On a personal level, the CEO DNA Code of operations is self-accountability. You set your dream, your expectation, and your hope to where you want to go. You apply the administrative abilities that have already been prewired within you and you write your vision down and make it plain so that YOU may run with it. But therein can be found the key—YOU must be the one to run with it. By the way, build a team around you that wants to run with you instead of holding you back.

On a personal level, the CEO DNA Code of operations is self-accountability.

I have a good friend who is a great teacher. I have watched her quietly sit at a table by herself only to be completely surrounded in a matter of minutes! People are drawn to her like a magnet. She will begin talking and people will pull up chairs three rows deep just to hear what she will impart. And yet, there are so many within her sphere of influence they will never have the opportunity to hear her words because of the lack of operations. Although my dear friend carries such an ability to teach, she struggles with the day-to-day operations, and therefore, people are in essence robbed of valuable insights from her life.

Her CEO DNA Codes are so evident when it comes to administration. She has vision, she has lists, and has even outlined the steps that need to take place in order to make her vision a reality. Nonetheless, the vision lies dormant in paper form only. The transition from administration to operations with the systems and the procedures and understanding of how everything will flow is ready, but it has not been activated! The switch inside continues to backfire because of the misunderstanding that only one CEO DNA Code is needed.

Operations will take away your excuses and expose truth. If you don't like what you see, you are responsible to change it!

As women, we have not been created as a one-dimensional, one-switch, one-code being. Rather, we have been created from birth as fully capable CEOs impregnated with every molecule of these areas: administration, operations, sales/marketing, and finances DNA. All are needed to complete the job.

This doesn't mean that we don't gather information and glean wisdom from others. The ability to receive and implement wise counsel is a sign of maturity. So it is in our best interest to gather around us men and women who together can create a strong synergy and push the vision to even greater levels. Yet at the end of the day, when push comes to shove and we review our actions, our operations and the ability to accomplish tasks reveal the truth of our efforts. Operations will take away your excuses and expose truth. If you don't like what you see, you are responsible to change it!

Now, even though the area of operations is about the task at hand and getting things done, it is often executed in the background without much fanfare. Most people won't even notice; it may seem tedious and is seldom a glamorous job! But without effective and efficient operations, nothing lasting or productive is accomplished. Plans simply remain dreams that never have the unction and sweat equity to become a reality.

You've already learned about administration. Let's contrast administration and operations:

> **Administration.** It's the ability to assess the situation and create systems and procedures for information or finances to flow from one area to another.

> **Operations.** It's the hands-on application of taking the instructions and applying them to the task in order to bring the desired outcome. In essence, the area of operations is doing what you know to do and doing it consistently.

As women, we have been created with the ability to not only create plans of strategy through our CEO DNA code of administration, but we also carry the innate ability to bring forth and birth the accomplishment! We are not called to live a life that is pregnant with promise but never has a due date. There must be a time of delivery, and that time is now!

Are you ready? Then strap on your heels because here we go....

Having an Effective Operations Plan

Goal setting leads to implementation. It is the marriage of administrative strategy with operations functionality. At first it can seem daunting, but as with anything, consistent application brings results. Stay focused, on track, and persistent—don't quit!

In my household, goal setting started by accident and over time evolved into a lifestyle. In the beginning, whenever my husband and I would travel, we would discuss our dreams. Soon we learned to categorize them and create plans to complete them. By the time my children were four years old, our goal setting patterns were established.

I remember my daughter Stephanie's first goal chart. She was four and said she wanted to pray for sixty seconds every day, stop being cranky, and save one dollar every year! It was hard, but she learned the importance of goal setting. To this day, Stephanie can be found with a day planner or electronic tablet outlining her progress. She has become a strong woman, well aware of the ingrained CEO DNA Codes within her.

Every year our family takes one week where we lift off the limitations of life and begin to concentrate on dreaming. We turn off the TV and instead of living vicariously through television drama, we begin to visualize what life could be like if money were no object, if time could not hinder, and if we really had the ability to live a life by design. Here's the process:

Day 1. The first day is always fun for us; lots of talking and laughing as we imagine all the toys and goodies, homes, and yachts that we would buy each other. We describe in detail the elegant foods we would eat, clothes we would buy, and jewelry we would own. We cut out pictures of cars and sailboats, RVs, and trailers until we end up with a pile of material goods. It's a fun day, but not truly satisfying.

Day 2. The next day we move past materialism and contemplate what our actions would be if we already owned everything we had cut out and placed in our materialistic pile and we still had vast wealth. We ask:

- How would we spend it?
- What relationships would we cultivate?

- What would we lavish upon our parents, grand-parents, relatives, and loved ones?
- How could we treat them?

Then the discussion grows to our communities and we describe the various ways that we could help each family. We cry as we think of how many lives would be changed as families come home and find letters in their mailboxes stating their mortgages have been paid in full. We imagine calling the credit card companies and paying off hundreds of thousands of dollars and providing them debt freedom.

Day 3. By the third day, we have moved far beyond materialistic goals. We have moved past personal and family wants, met the needs of extended loved ones, addressed hurts within our communities, and now we sit together as a family talking about how to bring lasting change. We envision college funds at local high schools, buying businesses, and training up a generation of entrepreneurs. We talk about foundations, legacy, and lasting impact.

Day 4. Now, we bring the white board to the family room and we begin to write down the dreams that have surfaced over the last three days. As we fill the board with all the ideas, we begin to discern the specific goals for this year. Out of all the dreams and desires that we have written, which are the ones that had lasting impact? What are our individual and family assignments for the year?

Day 5. After a good night's sleep we begin as a family to categorize and evaluate the goals.

Personal Goals

Physical. What do we need to implement in regards to our health to have the stamina to accomplish the vision for our lives?

Spiritual. I realize that we cannot make ourselves spiritually grow. However, if we apply the right spiritual food to our spirits and walk in the revelation, growth should be a by-product.

Financial. This is not a goal to cultivate the love of money. Rather, it is the monitoring of proper stewardship and cultivating resources needed for advancement.

Emotional. Emotional intelligence is a critical component for every individual, especially women. For too long we have used the excuse of emotionalism as a pass to act without discipline and restraint. We must mature past this misconception.

Material. Believe it or not, we are allowed to have a car that runs every time we turn the key, a house that is beautiful, and material possessions. It is only when those possessions own us that we cross the line. Every year I would put down a new kitchen on my goal list…it took ten years, but it finally happened!

Work. If we are to have influence, then we must be present in our homes and in the marketplace.

Relationship Goals

Yourself. Let me just start by saying that it is okay to take time for yourself and to have personal goals. You cannot lead people where you have never been, and if you expect those around you to grow, then you must grow as well! Women, invest in yourselves. So often women use all their time and energy investing in others that they have nothing left to invest in themselves. I exhort you to remember the commercial slogan, "You're worth it!"

Spouse. As women we tend to find identity through the acceptance of other people. If the people we love are also accepted by others, we also find acceptance. I married George when I was eighteen and I wanted him to be perfect so that everyone would like him, and in essence, they would like me. I remember that I always interrupted him and would finish his sentences because I didn't think he talked fast enough or smooth enough. I wanted to make sure it was perfect so people would like him.

Then I realized how demeaning it was when I wouldn't let my husband speak for himself. I realized I wasn't correcting him because I really cared about him; it was because I cared about *me*. I wanted to make sure *I* was accepted. It took me years of placing that goal on my annual list in order for me to break that habit; to truly edify him in public and allow him the freedom to be human and love every minute of it.

Children. I have three children, and as you can imagine, each of them are so different! Not only in personalities, but also in how they express and receive love. One of the smartest decisions I made while raising my children was reading a book called *The Five Love Languages* by Gary Chapman. This book helped me understand that when Mel and George would come and sit by me and just talk, they were giving and receiving love by our quality time together. However, my middle child, Stephanie, would view that as wasting time! She would much rather receive an act of service where she could do something for you and you would do something for her! If I tried the wrong method of showing love, they didn't understand or receive it. I needed to learn how they needed to receive love and become effective in delivering that to them.

Every year my goals include understanding my children even more. I encourage you to take time to really evaluate your relationship with your children and where you would like it to go. If you don't have children, then evaluate your relationship with a spouse or loved ones.

Community. There are so many open doors within a community: school boards, PTA, town council, local continuing education classes, nursing homes, community shelters, and food pantries. The list could go on and on. The key is to understand the purpose and design for your hometown. It is not an accident that you live there. You have a skill set, a CEO DNA Code within you that is in direct correlation to the cry of the land. Discover the cry, identify the need, align your resources, and redeem the land!

Once we have categorized everything, we begin to self-examine our motives and our commitment to what is written in front of us. Are we willing to pay the price, as an individual and as a team? If not, then it is erased, because it was never a goal but only a dream.

Day 6. When Day 6 arrives, our administration begins to flow. A strategy is created that upon implementation, will bring the desired results. We create a flowchart of responsibilities and actions that will need to take place. We determine what needs to be accomplished each month, each week, and each day. This is where systems and procedures shine! These are important elements of structure, especially on days where one grows weary.

Day 7. This is an excitingly somber day. We have accepted the call to battle and have determined to complete the course before us. Some courses will be for one year, others will be five years, ten years, and lifelong. We begin the process of picking up the battle plan for each goal and then step forth in a "Commitment of Operations" to advance the vision of the house. Each member of the family is instinctively aware of the independent actions required, and the magnitude of the calling serves to awaken interdependence upon each other. We are united in individual callings for the advancement of our household, knowing full well that when we gather next year to review our accomplishments, great endurance of skilled operations will have been displayed.

I realize that not every family can take a week away to establish personal, family, and community goals. In fact, when my children were under the age of five we never went on a vacation, but rather accomplished goal setting at home. But there comes a time in your life where you awaken to all that life has for you, your household, and your sphere of influence. Grab hold of all your desires and strategically apply "Administration for Advancement" and "Operations for Completion." Be determined to activate the CEO DNA Codes within you as well.

Grab hold of all your desires and strategically apply "Administration for Advancement" and "Operations for Completion." Be determined to activate the CEO DNA Codes within you as well.

You may think: "Crystal, you don't understand. This generation doesn't want a goal or another to-do list. If I try to do this with my family or workplace, it will never work." Okay, so start with you! Begin to take the personal responsibility to come into the full stature of all you were created to be!

Recently, I was thinking about how a child is born and despite its small size and the inability to communicate or take care of itself, within that child already lay the seeds for everything needed for the future. As parents we don't have to "rebirth" them every year; we simply need to draw out of them the essence of what is placed within them. We literally guide them as they evolve into a mature individual.

As women, we are no different. Everything we need is already written in codes within us! Those CEO DNA Codes vary in the degrees of maturity for each woman, yet they are still there. We must pull from within ourselves the essence of what is already placed within us, wrap it around us, and then confidently move forward!

Taking Our CEO DNA Codes Outside Our Homes

In regards to those around us, people don't want another list of responsibilities. We live in a fast-paced society and we don't need another thing to do. However, people are looking for purpose. Generation X is looking for a cause to be a part of; they want to know that they matter, that they have a purpose. Using the CEO DNA Codes of administration and operations can instill vision and provide a pathway for fulfillment. They just need someone to lead the way!

Now, I will warn you that if you are serious about awakening the CEO DNA codes within yourself and you cultivate those seeds and provide yourself the freedom and the attention needed to grow, you will change. That can be a scary concept not only to you, but also to those who love you! As you change, your actions will cause those around you to either disconnect or to embrace change as well. Do not let fear of others' expectations hold you back from stepping forth, but rather, run full force into all that has been designed for your life. The time for pretending to be alive is over; you have been given permission to really live!

Ask Yourself...

- What operations have you set into place in your home and workplace that effectively implement the administrative strategies you have planned?
- A key to operations is having a time of strategizing and planning. What do you need to do to set aside a few days or a week to set up the operations needed for the coming months and year?
- What hinders you from setting goals and then implementing operations for reaching them—fear, procrastination, laziness, distractions, _____ (you fill in the blank)? How will you eliminate these hindrances?

Women's Attire Sends a Message

Women want to be taken seriously and recognized for having more to offer than just our looks. We have the codes within us that, if properly cultivated, can escalate us to positions of great influence and culture change. While there is a desire to reflect our feminine side through our outward presentation, learning to dress with class that embraces and accentuates our beauty, without encouraging unwanted advances or causing tension in the office, is a skill that can reap many benefits.

Chapter 5

CEO Code of Sales/Marketing: Create the Culture!

Recently I attended an extended due diligence meeting in order to secure more investment professionals for Crystal Clear Finances. I had heard about an international company that had been overseeing pension plans for established companies within the United States for years. Since I was currently researching investment companies that could help me in the areas of actively managing my clients' accounts, this seemed like a great opportunity. I had completed my preliminary due diligence study by visiting their website and attending a local presentation of their marketing and administration tools. I even received continuing education credits because of the depth of investment and informational training they had provided. They were cutting-edge in every department: administration, operations, sales/marketing, and finances. Needless to say, I was sufficiently impressed!

I was hopeful that after my lengthy journey to their home office, I would have a new arrow for my quiver. This connection would be an impressive tool that I could add to my ever-growing arsenal of investment strategies. Not only would I be able to continue to weekly manage and oversee all my clients' accounts, but I would also have an internationally recognized company that had been in existence and managing money longer than I had been alive. Their international insight and experience in the global markets could provide yet another layer of protection and excellence for our clientele.

This potential addition to Crystal Clear Finances was strategic to providing the expanding services my clientele deserved. In this day and age, wisdom requires that clients' accounts be monitored on a weekly basis, instead of receiving the traditional quick perusal done once a quarter by many advisors. Because our office is on the cutting edge of this service, the investment firms that can align with our expectations are few, which explained the reason for my excitement.

I had narrowed down the already slim choices to three large investment firms. Since I had analyzed their complete operation, was pleased with the results, and found everything on the outside looking good, it was time for the "white glove" inspection. I accepted their invitation and drove out to their home office. I was joining approximately thirty-five other financial planners for a more in-depth look at their company.

Visiting a company that is trying to be hired for their services is the courtship phase in every professional relationship. Both parties want to look good, so the best image is projected, cobwebs are cleaned, desks straightened, and everyone is on their best behavior. Even the topics, speakers, and progression of introductions are intentional. Investment companies usually have one-and-a-half days to convey their vision and DNA to prospective advisors. Every topic is strategically positioned with the hope of securing the advisor's business. This trip was no different.

As I pulled up to their campus located on pristine farmland, I was impressed by the numerous windows, the shape of the buildings, and the clean, open ambience presented. The trees were shaped elegantly, the grass cut to the accepted height, and walkways were manicured, clean, and inviting. Everything on the outside spoke of a combination between investment success and a wholesome farm community. I hurriedly parked my car and headed towards the door, confident that this was going to be enlightening and fun!

As I entered their lobby, I grabbed a quick glance of the room. Before I could evaluate more, I was greeted by four of their top team members, each dedicated to serving me and securing my business. Dressed in business casual, they emitted an understated posture of confidence that what they had to offer, would not be refused. I had entered their sphere of influence and they were secure in their product.

At each hurried glance, the hairs began to twitch on the back of my neck. Excitement turned to confusion and then dread.

As they quickly ushered me through the lobby and towards the conference room where everyone was to gather, I tried to slow my pace; I wanted to savor the essence of my surroundings. At each hurried glance, the hairs began to twitch on the back of my neck. Excitement turned to confusion and then dread.

My quick survey brought my eyes past the first impression of openness to the actual items being displayed. On the far side of the room, leaning against the wall was a fifteen-foot industry stock cardboard airplane crumpled in a heap. The cockpit was intact but the wings were broken, the propeller smashed, and the remaining pieces strategically placed in a five-foot diameter around the display. I slowed my step, turned to my guide, and raised an eyebrow. He chuckled softly and replied, "Artwork."

We turned a corner and to the left beyond the tables of hors d'oeuvres and assorted beverages, there was an actual ice cream truck in the lobby! This amused me; after all, an ice cream truck in the lobby? I could understand that type of "artwork!" Yet, as I looked closer, instead of windows there were steel plates with machine guns sticking out of them. I stopped and read the front of the truck. The title read, "I Scream Truck." Every warning bell inside me began to blare. I knew this ship was going down and I didn't want to be on it.

I asked politely where the bathroom was, and with a look of innocence in their eyes, they pointed behind me to an entrance by the picture. I could feel my sweat beginning to surface. I hesitantly turned, praying that there would be some normalcy in what I would see next.

From where I stood, I could just make out a green outline of a picture over three feet in diameter. As each echoing step drew me closer, clarity came and the dots began to fill in. Finally I stood by the women's bathroom door staring at a woman covered by a green ski mask. The openings showed eyes wide with fright and her lipstick lips outlining the gasp of horror. Beside this portrait, nailed to the wall was the proud title, "Robbed."

I found myself trembling, partly in disgust and partly in anger. A feeling much similar to finding a perfect apple, only to bite inside and see half a worm; you realize you have already swallowed half and you want to dislodge the first half while throwing the second half as far away as possible.

I spent the next four hours watching them parade the top executives from each division across the stage. I listened politely as they presented their "spiel" regarding the strength of their departments and how they could help my clients become even more successful. They showed statistics and research that validated their claims. There was no way to deny that they were technically and intellectually skilled at what they did. Yet, in my ears, the DNA of destruction and the culture it created drowned out their muted sounds of progress.

As we finished the afternoon presentation and prepared to leave for dinner, they took us on a tour of the existing artwork in their facility. Their pride and connection to these offensive works of art revealed their fascination with devastation and the depths of destruction that was connected to their soul.

Every piece of art implied or flagrantly showcased torture, destruction, and despair— especially to women.

A quick turn and one flight of stairs took us to their investment floor. Once the entry card was swiped, we were escorted into their trading room. Uniformed desks lined the floor; each one bore the same stark resemblance and was connected to a coil that fed down from a large wiring harness that overlooked the length of the room. Our guide explained that every desk received their source of power from this system, which they affectionately dubbed, "The Python."

As dinner began, I sat with one of the younger employees and asked how she gained employment with this company and what it was like working here. She explained that while attending college, she was recruited. They said her degree would be helpful but was not mandatory. What they desired most was the ability to "accept and cultivate the culture" within the company. When I pressed her to describe what she meant, she pointed to the artwork and explained that this was their "culture." Every piece of art implied or

flagrantly showcased torture, destruction, and despair—
especially to women.

The key point and common thread between all the artwork and Python labeling was that it had been handpicked,
constructed, and displayed by the president and founder of
the company and his daughter. Throughout the entire com-
pound, this culture of blatant disrespect had effectively
been displayed.

**Culture is the intangible embodiment
of our beliefs, values, and purposes. It is invisible
and yet can be brought into tangible existence through
the choreographed infusion of marketing.**

Culture is the intangible embodiment of our beliefs,
values, and purposes. It is invisible and yet can be brought
into tangible existence through the choreographed infusion
of marketing. Culture in itself is neither good nor bad; it
is dependent upon the belief system that is supporting it.
These beliefs and values can either be healthy or unhealthy.
In the example above, we see the impact of negative values
and the culture it created. However, we have the opportunity to create positive culture. Positive culture demands
that character and values be displayed. We can bring integrity back into business dealings, faithfulness into relationships, and compassion to our communities.

Effective marketing is the bridge for establishing culture and can help transition an individual from observing,
to embracing, to endorsement. Those who remain ignorant to its power default to promotional puppets endorsing the culture through their silence. Silence is a form of
acceptance. Therefore, it is vital that we understand how

culture is created and the strategy of connecting the Sales/ Marketing CEO Code.

As women, we subconsciously wield this gift of influence into every atmosphere we enter. Our actions, words, and even nonverbal presentations evoke a sound and emit a message that paves the way before us. However, if we are to effectively use this influence to create productive change, both in our home and in the business realm, then creating culture must become intentional. Personal culture, family atmosphere, and the business realm are in desperate need of culture change. We must define the culture we desire and then use every marketing tool available for awakening, enforcing, and expanding culture.

Personal Culture

In order to accomplish culture correction by injecting our CEO Codes into our sphere of influence, there must be an intentional game plan of implementation. We must begin to realize that every component of what we do creates a message. There are no wasted actions or words. We are constantly endorsing or dismantling an atmosphere. We must therefore ask ourselves, what message are we trying to convey? What is our voice; what is our sound?

Once you understand your culture, you can learn the avenues in which your sound and message can be introduced, reinforced, and multiplied. Marketing opens the door for your culture to be introduced, accepted, and expanded. It is the presentation of who you are, your direction, and a definition of the impact you are seeking to create.

We have defined culture as atmosphere and marketing as the tools used to expand the atmosphere. These marketing tools can be used in all realms of a woman's life and can correlate directly with words and behavior. Behavior is the outward expression of an inward conviction.

Women that are unsure of themselves and their identity tend to project a hesitancy regarding their femininity. They are uncomfortable with who they are and project that timidity within their culture. Timidity tends to adapt to the current culture, regardless of its origin. Likewise, those who accept and find comfort within their own skin enjoy who they are, despite challenges along the way. Those who walk in confidence tend to influence the culture around them. You have a choice every day as to what you are going to promote and allow into your life and what you will dismiss. You will continually teach the people around you how to treat you by the way you project yourself.

Personal development is a key to growing in acceptance of yourself and others. However, when you are creating your marketing plan for life and dreaming of the possibilities, you will face the decision and pressure to downsize and adapt to the culture around you. Yet, trying to live a vision that already has all the answers and requires maintenance instead of growth is not vision—it is stagnation.

There are guidelines in how you promote culture. Single women, mothers, wives, and businesswomen must be aware that there are sensitive areas of marketing that need to be addressed. Let me make the following suggestion, especially for women already working in the business realm. It has been said, "A moment on the lips, forever on the hips." We have accepted this statement as dealing with the food we put into our mouths. I would like to be bold enough to make a slight adjustment here and focus instead on what comes out of our mouths as opposed to what goes into them.

Because men are visually and verbally stimulated, women need to be aware of all aspects of their marketing. Both our dress and speech will provide access or rejection of sexual advancement. If we are not careful, we can self-sabotage our attempts to gain respect by the common mistake known as the "slip of the lips!" Coarse jesting and crude watercooler talk may have been fun and acceptable in high school, but in the real world of professional business, it is time to elevate your vocabulary to a new level. It is a slippery slope when you choose to use your femininity as your ace card in the workplace. All it takes is a few moments of sexual innuendos or suggestions, and you have taken the focus from the creativity and genius of your mind and shifted it to your hips. Once you have allowed the shift to happen, good luck on getting the focus back up where it belongs.

So we might rephrase the cliché to be, "Once through the lips, focus is forever on the hips." Value yourself enough to guard your lips from self-sabotaging your advancement. Remember, we are the ones who will teach others how to treat us and where we have drawn the line in the sand.

Learning to dress with class that embraces and accentuates our beauty, without encouraging unwanted advances or causing tension in the office, is a skill that can reap many benefits.

Women want to be taken seriously and recognized for having more to offer than just our looks. We have the codes within us that, if properly cultivated, can escalate us to positions of great influence and culture change. While there is a desire to reflect our feminine side through our outward presentation, learning to dress with class that embraces and accentuates our beauty, without encouraging unwanted advances or causing tension in the office, is a skill that can reap many benefits.

Our Appearance Markets Our Character

Now let's expand this concept past the office and into our personal lives, our homes, and our communities. Ask yourself these questions: Did you ever have a provocatively-dressed woman walk by your husband and you knew he couldn't help notice how beautiful she was? Did that make you want to pursue initiating a relationship with that woman, or did you breathe more comfortably the further she walked away from you?

Part of marketing is our appearance. As women, we appreciate working and interacting with wholesome, quality, good-looking individuals. However, when the line is crossed in regards to questionable or suggestive behavior, the walls go up and the focus shifts to protecting. If your goal is to present yourself as a beautiful, competent, caring woman who is secure in herself, her marriage, her home, and her work environment, then there is a way for you to walk in beauty and confidence. This will draw others to you instead of from you. It does not mean that you diminish yourself for others, but rather it means that your persona intentionally draws others to your level.

We should seek to impress our colleagues and clients with our intelligence, competence, and thoughtfulness by letting our inner qualities supersede our outward marketing adornments.

I know that when I work with clients, I do my best to look professional and feminine at the same time. I enjoy being a woman and I am not interested in the lie that pressures women to trade their identity in order to be successful in a man's world. I learned that I can be an influential businesswoman and still keep my curls; and I can enjoy dressing up in high heels! This world does not belong just to men; it is for both men *and* women. Women complement and complete the picture. However, our choice of attire should display a respect in knowing who we are while working to connect with other women around us. Let me emphasize this. We should seek to impress our colleagues and clients with our intelligence, competence, and thoughtfulness by letting our inner qualities supersede our outward marketing adornments.

Culture Setting in the Home

On the family front, understanding your marketing CEO DNA Code is equally as critical. As wives and parents we are continually sending a message into the atmosphere within our household. We have direct correlation to our personal, marriage, and household culture. Hence the ever-popular saying, "If Momma ain't happy, ain't nobody happy"! This begs the question of whether you realize the purpose of your home environment, and if you are intentionally creating it. Is it a place where you, your spouse, and children are refueled? Is it a team environment or adversarial in nature? Have you effectively turned your house into a home?

In our home, we have intentionally established a culture. We have created an environment of personal development, safety, ethics, moral values, and unconditional love. This culture has been experienced by many of our children's friends. Those who have chosen to embrace it refer to us as Mama and Papa Bear. They in return, have become affectionately accepted as our "cubs."

I remember one night when one of our "cubs" called in a panic. There was physical violence in his home, and as a son, he couldn't take watching the abuse anymore. He had fought back and the police had been called. As we rushed to his home, we found a trembling young adult whose mask of disinterest and bravado had been dislodged. We eventually brought him home, the house quieted down, and soon he drifted off to sleep. I remember lying there, listening as he slept in safety, thankful that he had been able to walk into an atmosphere of acceptance which had been cultivated years ago.

The next day as family and friends were notified, the phrase at the end of each call stated: "You should come here; it is so safe, so welcoming. I haven't slept so good and felt such peace in a real long time." I realize that not every family experiences physical danger and abuse, but many homes serve only to cultivate uninterested lives of survival, each individual struggling for direction in a home only one step safer than the streets. Teenagers hide in their rooms while parents work in their offices or glaze over in front of the television. There is no active cultivation of personal and family goals. No instruction or guidance is given to help bring children and even spouses into the fullness of what they were created to become. Instead of homes being a launching pad and refueling station, they have become a setting that aborts destinies across this nation.

We must awaken the marketing codes within us and learn to create an atmosphere conducive for growth.

As women, we are not just thermometers! We set the temperature of our lives, our marriages, our homes, and business arenas. We must awaken the marketing codes within us and learn to create an atmosphere conducive for growth. This can be accomplished through verbal interaction and proper physical touch between family members and our spouse. Marketing at home also includes sights and sounds within the home and working at understanding one another, combined with the goal to see each other advance.

This marketing challenge can seem daunting and perhaps unattainable, but in reality, as we unlock the codes within us to embrace the person we were created to be, we establish a comfort zone within our homes. This creates a platform in which we are no longer threatened by one other and which fosters an environment that will help us, and those we love, to soar. As spouses grow in their own security, they learn not to be threatened by their partner. Additionally, families embrace and create a culture within their home that promotes acceptance and advancement, allowing the community and territory to be influenced.

Behavior Markets Who We Are

Whether as a single woman, a mother, a wife, a business realm influencer, or a combination of them, you must be willing to believe that you have the right to awaken the codes within you and experience the fullness of womanhood. So go ahead and dream, but understand that once you commit to a dream, the journey will cost you! You will be required not only to activate the codes of administration and operations, but also a full-fledged plan of marketing. Your marketing plan, like everything else, should be intentional, continuous, growing, evolving, and constantly reinventing itself.

Your sphere of influence will continue to change over time, and you are required to continually adapt your methods of presentation. Knowing your message and your key foundational strategies for marketing will allow you to implement adjustments in the midst of trying times. In other words, master the basics so that you can adapt them in the heat of the battle.

> **Your marketing plan, like everything else, should be intentional, continuous, growing, evolving, and constantly reinventing itself.**

The cost for your dreams and culture advancement will be more than you thought and requiring expenditures sooner rather than later. When self-pity comes, you must choose to give up the perceived right to wilt and wallow. You may be tempted to quit by believing the lies that you don't have enough money, time, support, skill, or strength to carry on. Instead, be willing to take responsibility for your decisions and have the courage to lead. Learning about leadership doesn't put anything on the line, but living leadership puts everything on the line. It is time that your marketing code awakens and you live a life that is intentional! Life is transformed by one empowered choice at a time; you can do it!

> **The cost for your dreams and culture advancement will be more than you thought and requiring expenditures sooner rather than later.**

Women are in the marketing business. What we wear, how we act, how we dress, our attention or lack of attention to detail, all create a voice that is continually echoing, even if you can't hear it. My challenge to you is to awaken the CEO DNA Code of marketing that is within you. Discover the image you want to portray, define your message, and strategize how you will implement culture change. It is time for your voice to be heard!

Ask Yourself...

1. Describe the culture you create personally and professionally.

2. How would your family describe your marketing? Is it consistent?

3. What is the message you are trying to convey?

4. What skill sets and tools do you use to create your voice?

5. What is your response to the updated version of, "Once through the lips, forever on the hips?"

6. Do you use your femininity as a weapon or as manipulation at home, in the workplace, or your community?

7. Do other women feel threatened by the way that you dress and carry yourself?

8. How have you learned to combine your femininity with professionalism?

9. What steps do you have in place for personal development?

The Key to Wealth

When it comes to finances, women often overlook a key financial truth. The absence of this revelation has kept many women from transitioning from riches to true wealth. This key is in understanding that the true financial goal for work is never about making a paycheck to pay your expenses and create a lifestyle. The financial purpose for your job, work, or career is to create income so that you can buy assets and build wealth.

Chapter 6

CEO Code of Finance:
Cash Is Queen

The heat was unbearable. I doubled over and placed my hands on my knees for a short, well-deserved rest. Running up and down the soccer field in the humid, sticky days of summer did not seem like a wise decision today! A shrill whistle pierced the air and brought me back to the game as the ball came back in play and headed my way. I watched as it bounced from the throw-in and headed straight towards me. "Ahh," I thought, "the opportunity for me to score and validate my position on the team." As I began darting forward, eyes intent on the ball, a black pair of cleats swooped in, took possession of the ball and knocked me, and my visions of victory, to the ground. The rest of the game grew fuzzy as I determined to find the owner of those cleats to introduce him to mine! Five years passed and I traded in my white cleats for a white dress and married my soccer ball sweetheart, who just happened to be the owner of that black pair of cleats!

I anticipated that marriage with George would be a ball! What I never expected was the tug-of-war that would escalate between my white-collar expectations and his blue-collar realities. My father had held prestigious titles, including Senior Vice President, of a well-established, national bank. He was instrumental in creating intellectual property and designing computer programs back in the late 1970s. My father-in-law was a third-generation truck driver; stable, consistent, and hard working. In both households, our mothers were stay-at-home moms, fully supported by their husbands. Due to my father's paycheck, I lived in an 8,400-square-foot home with my eleven brothers and sisters, while George's family of four lived in a comfortable but much smaller home. George's lifestyle was markedly different from mine. Clearly our definitions of financial provision and advancement were not going to be the same!

For the first few years there was financial surplus every week, which I promptly spent and saved very little. Life was developing nicely and we ignorantly took the next step in the American Dream. We bought a 4,600-square-foot home. It was then that the lessons in finances began! We used every penny to purchase our home, and as long as we made the $1,279-a-month payment for the next thirty years and there were no unexpected expenses, we would be fine. We could afford a place to live, but there was no extra room to breathe!

In our excitement to be homeowners, we had pushed for a quick closing. This meant moving in January in what turned out to be one of the worst snowstorms New York had experienced in years. We soon discovered that due to the fact that our farmhouse was built over two hundred years ago, it had no insulation in the walls. This translated into purchasing one hundred gallons of fuel a week. We learned to dress in multiple layers, donned our hats and socks, and still shivered in the cold. Our goal was to keep the house warm enough so nothing would freeze, including the children!

Since we had made the mistake of using all our cash reserves to purchase the home, we attempted to maintain our existence from one paycheck to another. With the price of oil, utility costs for a large home, and the introduction of a mortgage payment into our budget, in just a few short months, we had fallen behind. Three months later our largest customer went bankrupt, and the company that purchased their holdings had their own trucking company and no longer needed our services. We scrambled to find additional work to keep our company afloat. We had to pay our employees on credit card cash advances. Then we stopped all paychecks to ourselves, but nothing seemed to work. We had no choice but to close the trucking company.

**What a difference a year had made—
from the palace to the pit in one easy slide!**

What a difference a year had made—from the palace to the pit in one easy slide! Since we owned the trucking company, there was no unemployment and therefore no income. We pulled our children out of private school, began home schooling and started babysitting for a dollar an hour. George gave up the dream of owning his own business and took a job to ensure our survival.

Our second winter came and since we couldn't afford fuel, we began to heat our home with wood stoves. We had three of them going at all times and burned one and a half cords of wood a week. We redefined the meaning of the word "sledding." The object was to go out into the woods and find any twig, branch, or log, load it onto the sled, and race back to the house as quickly as possible, bring it in by the stove, and then repeat as needed. George's schedule consisted of going to work at 4:00 p.m., arriving home around

6:00 a.m., cutting enough wood to get us through the day, and then sleeping until he had to leave for work again.

At this point in our financial lives, we existed on thirty-five dollars a week for food, while keeping the mortgage just one payment from foreclosure. Every month we alternated between paying lights or the telephone. Spring and summer came and the car hauling company where George worked decided to go on strike. Strike pay was thirty-five dollars a week. This lasted for six weeks. When winter came, we closed off all the rooms in the house except four. Our pipes froze that year and despair set in. We had no hope, no purpose, and no way out.

At this point in our financial lives, we existed on thirty-five dollars a week for food, while keeping the mortgage just one payment from foreclosure.

Another summer came and went without much change, and when winter entered the scene, our water pipes broke, the hot water heater went, and the motor in the car blew. We spoke with a financial counselor and they declared the situation hopeless and strongly advised filing for bankruptcy. It was a quiet ride home from their office, both of us digesting the prognosis of our situation. They had pronounced a death sentence that we had worked three years to avoid. The financial battle had been long and weary and we were emotionally empty, disconnected, and completely disillusioned with life. I mechanically followed my husband into the breakfast room, waiting for the shell shock to wear off. George leaned forward and slumped down on the dining room table. I watched helplessly as his small dark eyes finally allowed tears to escape and the little boy within emerged, "I can't."

"Can't what?" I probed.

"I can't declare bankruptcy."

The statement hung in the air as inwardly we wrestled with the professional guidance we had received versus the years of battle we had already put into this fight. Resolve was shaking and the decision made from this point forward would affect the course of our lives significantly. Silence continued to dominate, except for the methodical clicking of our battery-operated clock. We were in countdown.

I looked at the beaten man before me. Gone was the little boy who had tried to tame the world; he had barely enough strength to throw in the towel. Deep within me the resolve started to bubble. I defiantly stood up and declared, "We will continue to fight. If it takes all our lives to beat this, I would rather fight for one day of financial freedom then to surrender to the slavery of debt forever. We will win this war our way."

I would like to say that at that moment, money floated down from heaven, all the bills disappeared, and everything changed, but it didn't. We still received harassing phone calls from the credit card companies, food was sparse, and heating the home was an ever-consuming battle. Yet, with that verbal resolution, something shifted inside. We were ready for round two.

This time we shifted from the mindset of survival to one of strategy. We went back to the professionals and asked for a plan. They said that if we made all the payments listed, we could be debt-free in just five years. We took their plan and began to read books and educate ourselves regarding the financial realm. Instead of focusing on where we were, we began to learn about where we wanted to go! We increased our skill sets and began changing our mindsets. We would not be victims; we would be leaders. We refused to be defined by our current situation and began setting and implementing goals of development.

Things continued to be tight, but they were changing, and we had help along the way. I remember how one neighbor, Dick Keel, would come down with his John Deere tractor filled with a big bucket load of wood, asking if we would mind using it up for him! And every Christmas morning for four years, a woman from church would stop by with a gift for each one of my children. The blessings seemed few and far between, but we were grateful for each one.

Three years later, by the grace of God, the five-year plan was completed early. From the time we purchased the home until the day we became debt-free was seven years! Once the debt was gone, there was now surplus. I knew we were approaching the moment that we had spent the last seven years preparing for. Had we learned our lesson? Would we repeat the cycle of poor financial habits and spending, or had we grown into financially savvy individuals? Yes, we were ready. We had learned that wealth must become a mindset before it shows up in your bank account.

In their eyes, I had no value. However, they were incorrect, because net worth does not determine my value!

Soon after we became debt-free, my sister called me and told me about a financial planner who offered free consultations. I was skeptical to go because I had tried to get help before, but no one had wanted to come close to me. In their eyes, I had no value. However, they were incorrect, because net worth does not determine my value! I decided to seek financial guidance regarding investing, and as I sat in the consultation, I understood from my reading what the financial planner was talking about. We were ready to advance! True to the statement that opportunity comes to those who are prepared, he turned to me and offered me a job. He told me he would pay for my training and the licenses that I would need and that he would mentor me. And then he said, "I have no idea why I am providing you this position." But I did. My time to financially soar had come!

As I learned more about finances, I wanted to start investing, but I knew from everything I had read that I needed to start saving first.

As I learned more about finances, I wanted to start investing, but I knew from everything I had read that I needed to start saving first. Yet, I felt behind the gun and needed to catch up. My concerns were similar to the thought processes of those who have suffered significant setbacks. I decided the wisest move would be to place eighty percent of the surplus into savings and place the remainder between life insurance and investments. Excited as I was to invest, I knew proper counsel was to build up a reserve first.

I was glad that I had ignored my emotions and had been diligent with my actions, because soon after, as I was sitting in church, I was approached by one of George's friends from work. He informed me that George had just been hit by a car, thrown thirty feet, and was on his way to the hospital. Thankfully, he was alive, conscious, and asking for me. As we sped towards the emergency room, fear and frustration trickled down, creating pathways on my face. It had only been two months since we had won the financial battle of our lives. Could we face another one so soon? In my mind I quickly calculated our savings, evaluated our emotional reserves, and waited with bated breath to see my husband. It was too close to call.

The prognosis was that his leg had been broken in two separate places and would take over four months to heal. During that recovery period, we lived on my income, workers' compensation, and the money I had placed into the savings account. Although it was financially tight, this was the best four months of our lives. The kids finally had time with their daddy again. They laughed, watched silly movies, played hours and hours of monopoly, and just plain loved on their dad. To this day, they always look back at that time as a special time just for them.

Since then, George has built a trucking company and I have gone on to receive numerous certifications in finance, become a Registered Investment Advisor and Certified Financial Planner™, and cultivated my own financial planning office. We now have heat in every room and have expanded our home to make room for all the neighborhood kids who find their way to our doorstep.

Managing Cash Flow

I share this story because as women each of us has faced our own financial battles with timetables that range from months to years. However, there are steps that can be taken during this process to help ensure that you are ready for the next level when the opportunity presents itself. One of the core foundational steps of advancement is to develop an understanding of finance principles. This starts with creating cash flow projections, which we can simply call a "budget." I have found that having a multitiered budget allows us to understand what is needed in regards to core survival income, then basic needs, and finally, a tier for the surplus. Too many times, we try to live in the outer tier of abundance when we haven't created the cash flow to sustain it.

I remember when my daughter Melonie was thirteen. She announced that she was ready to begin driving. I explained that just like everyone else in New York State, she had to wait until she was sixteen before she could go for her permit. She shook her head and patiently explained to me that she did not have to abide by this rule because her father was a fourth-generation truck driver, and since she was his daughter, she already had the skill set within her. She also hastened to add that she had been driving a tractor for a few years now and had become quite proficient! After chuckling softly to myself, I calmly explained to her that while she presented an interesting argument, if she started driving without her license and was pulled over by a policeman, they would not find her rationale as amusing as I did. In fact, by taking a shortcut now, she could ultimately end up postponing the day when she was legally allowed to drive.

Taking shortcuts because you feel the rules don't apply to your situation is a trap that can short-circuit your future, especially in the areas of finance.

Warning: *Don't take shortcuts.* Taking shortcuts because you feel the rules don't apply to your situation is a trap that can short-circuit your future, especially in the areas of finance. If you believe that you can live on the outer edge of surplus and enjoy the luxuries of vacations, eating out, and fulfilling your list of wants, and yet have to struggle to keep your basic bills paid on time, then you are working under the false illusion that your finances are under control. This doesn't mean that you won't be able to enjoy any of these things. It simply means that if you participate in this lifestyle before you have learned the financial skill sets needed to sustain them, then you will short-circuit your process and it will take you longer to ultimately reach the place of financial freedom.

Those who take time to create a budget, discipline themselves, become skilled in managing their finances, and then grow in their financial knowledge, will be able to move effectively and efficiently from the circle of "Core Survival." They will skim through the middle level of "Just Enough," and proceed immediately to the outer layer of "Surplus." The time delay between each circle level corresponds to the financial and emotional growth of each individual.

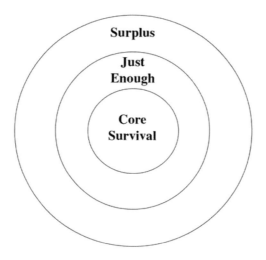

As women, it is important that we understand each of these circles and effectively learn to navigate between them, especially because statistics show that ninety percent of all women will face a period of time in their lives where they will be solely responsible for all the financial decisions within their households. Understanding finances empowers us and creates options so that we are not at the mercy of others. Too many women have been taken advantage of due to their lack of financial intelligence.

Perhaps one of the reasons why we struggle with finances is that we have been taught incorrectly about the purpose of finances. Growing up, society taught us that if we graduate from high school, we could get a job and make enough money to pay our bills. We would work somewhere for forty-five years and be a loyal employee who faithfully pays their living expenses.

If you were dissatisfied with this arrangement and found yourself to be an overachiever, then your other option was to graduate from high school and go to college. Having a college degree was the golden ticket to a higher-paying job with a corner office in some downtown high-rise! Your income would increase, as would the expenses associated with your improved lifestyle. Any funds left over from necessities could be spent on the finer things in life. Essentially, this is the same pattern as before: make a paycheck, pay your bills, and spend the surplus. Americans have become very experienced in living this cycle!

The Real Goal of Work!

When it comes to finances, women often overlook a key financial truth. The absence of this revelation has kept many women from transitioning from riches to true wealth. This key is in understanding that the true financial goal for work is never about making a paycheck to pay your expenses and create a lifestyle. The financial purpose for your job, work, or career is to create income so that you can buy assets and build wealth.

Step One: Creating an income source for cash flow and developing a budget. Working is simply Step Number One in the process of building wealth! However, women across this country have viewed this first step of having a job, business, or source of income as the only step, and nothing is further from the truth! Step One is creating income to buy assets.

Step Two: Investing in assets. Step Two is continuing to buy assets until the residual passive income from these assets creates an income stream that allows your job to be optional.

As women, we often leave finances to our husbands or other men deemed "more qualified." Your personal finances are a launching pad for your goals. They provide the fuel needed to have a successful liftoff. Allowing others to make your financial decisions without your substantial input can limit you in the long run. Have qualified counselors and a financial planner help with the due diligence needed for your investments can substantially mitigate risk.

Due to the stock market's performance over the past few years, many women feel they are not ready for retirement and so they are taking risks that hurt them over time. Always remember that there are "risks" and then there are "calculated risks." Knowing the difference between the two can make a major difference in your financial picture. You don't need to become a financial advisor, but remaining aware of your financial situation and creating a plan for where you are headed is important. And let me assure you, as a woman myself, you can do this!

Step Three: Create multiple streams of income. These streams of income can serve to not only allow you and your loved ones to enjoy the full spectrum of wealth and surplus that we discussed earlier, but it also creates a platform for community development, resources for inventions, and the advancement of the economy. Unfortunately, we were never taught this in school!

We believe the commercials on television that tell us "we are worth it" and that we should buy whatever we want, whenever we want, regardless of the resulting debt repercussions. We have bought into this lie because "liabilities" have been glorified and presented to look like "assets." Too often we purchase liabilities thinking that we are moving forward, while in reality we are slipping into debt and falling behind.

Too often we purchase liabilities thinking that we are moving forward, while in reality we are slipping into debt and falling behind.

In his book *Rich Dad Poor Dad*, Robert Kiyosaki provides a simple definition for this dilemma. Assets will feed you, and liabilities will eat you. If you look at your purchases, simply ask yourself if the long-term effect will provide income and feed you when you are no longer working, or if it will eat you by taking away the resources needed to sustain that "asset." This simple explanation can help to clarify and alleviate incorrect purchases.

In addition to learning the financial principle of budgeting and understanding cash flow, I recommend using one of the many software tools on the market that will allow you to see your personal balance sheet as well as your profit and loss statement. We tend to think this is strictly for business owners, yet being able to identify areas of overspending or unexpected increases in monthly operating expenses can help you reposition for a stronger financial position. Finances can only be spent in one of three places: 1) consumption by your lifestyle; 2) transference to others through bills and debt; and, 3) accumulation for the future.

A "profit and loss statement" helps to see which of these three categories are creating the largest pull on your resources. Simply put, a profit and loss statement is your income relative to your expenses. It will let you know on a daily basis the amount you are spending in each of the three categories noted above. If you notice that you are unable to save and invest at least ten percent of your income, then you can look at your P&L statement and identify what is draining your resources. This information can provide you insight for a plan to remove the debt and increase wealth. I remember the first year that I kept track of every expense. I was shocked at the amount I had spent on groceries. I made a decision right then and there that I was not going to "eat" away my retirement. I would find a way to cut back so that I could have the resources to enjoy my future.

Learning to read financial statements, understand the financial jargon of assets and liabilities, and create a sustainable financial plan are important steps towards financial independence. However, many women argue that this is not their area of expertise and that they are not equipped to handle finances. Yet, nothing could be further from the truth. We were created with the innate ability to reason and process information. In fact, we are classified as "multitaskers" who can facilitate several discussions at once! We can spot a sale a mile away and quickly calculate the savings from each purchase.

In order to cultivate the CEO DNA Code of finance within you and prepare for the next step of opportunity, mentoring will be required.

Cooking dinner and recalculating the measurements of each recipe is a minor struggle at first, but soon we fly through translating numbers and degrees with ease. Processing bills and balancing the checkbook are all tasks we are equipped to handle if we simply take the time to understand the process and create patterns of familiarity. After all, finances are simply a matter of numbers, logic, dreams, and strategy, and women are capable of handling each section with complete confidence and competence. This is evident through the increasing number of women who are the leading financial contributors within their home.

In order to cultivate the CEO DNA Code of finance within you and prepare for the next step of opportunity, mentoring will be required. You can achieve this through books you read, lessons you learn from others' mistakes, and by setting aside personal time to seek out those with expertise in the financial field. Be aware. They will be busy and you will need to be respectful of their time, but many successful financial planners and business-savvy individuals have reached a point where community investment and legacy building is part of their personal and professional goals.

What Are Your Future Goals?

This leads us to another critical point. You must have financial goals: personally, as a family unit, and as a company. Goals can be structured in accordance with the circles of cash flow, noted above. Your goals will all fall into three areas:

Goal #1: Cash flow, budgeting, and investing. You will have core needs for cash flow and investing that need to be achieved in order to create sustainability for future funding. These types of goals would include creating a working budget, becoming debt-free, creating your own infinite banking system, and the development of residual income streams. Also included is the intentional investing of financial resources on yourself, such as going back to college, hiring professional coaches for personal and business development, or providing funding to establish a business.

In this initial financial goal, it is critical to define exactly where you want to go and the resources needed to achieve this goal. This is not the time to be vague or to focus on everyone else except you. Just like the message heard on the airlines—you must first safely attach your own oxygen mask before assisting those around you! If you are moved with compassion too soon, you can end up taking the financial seed that would have created sustainable income and giving it to others. They will unintentionally eat the seeds for your future. Wisdom dictates that you first cultivate the seeds of wealth that are within your hand by defining and outlining a plan of growth. Once growth has stabilized, then you can move into the second goal.

Wisdom dictates that you first cultivate the seeds of wealth that are within your hand by defining and outlining a plan of growth. Once growth has stabilized, then you can move into the second goal.

Goal #2: Empowering your family, friends, and colleagues. The second goal will be helping those you love or those within your immediate sphere of influence to grow financially, emotionally, intellectually, and spiritually. Since the core financial needs of survival have been addressed and met within the first goal, this level allows resources to be directed towards expenses that can be defined more as a want than a need.

This realm also allows us to invest in our immediate loved ones without fear of disrupting the financial foundation of the first core goal. At this point, we sit down with our children and have them share their goals. Whether they are using their resources to pay for a master's degree, heading into another year of law school, or trying to buy a car, we determine the amount that can be applied to help support them in their pursuits. As a family unit we are aware of our limited resources and work to make sure each member is not thrown off track by the unexpected events of life.

Many times as women we want to financially help our loved ones and we disrupt our financial foundations in the process. It is important that we don't fall into the trap of believing that money is an expression of love. Money is simply a tool—nothing more and nothing less. Used effectively it can help provide an avenue of freedom and assistance to our loved ones. Used incorrectly, it can enslave a family to a lifestyle of credit card bondage and the perpetual churning of meaningless spending. One of the greatest gifts that we can provide to ourselves and our loved ones is financial intelligence. By using our CEO DNA Code of finance, we can continually evaluate our environment and our spending and make the required adjustments.

**Money is simply a tool—
nothing more and nothing less.**

Goal #3: Leaving a legacy and making a difference. The third goal is the realm of personal enjoyment, community impact, and influence. This last goal takes time to reach but we must always stay focused. Without such a focus our lives could stagnate due to excessive, self-centered consumption. By the time a person has reached this stage, they should have cultivated a residual income stream that would allow them to meet many of the needs within their community, while still planning for the income needs of future generations of family. The residual income could be through real estate purchases, investments, business opportunities, or inventions. Regardless of the means, there is a consistent pattern of long-term planning in place.

It has been said that when Bill Gates was building Microsoft, he did not give to charities. He explained that he needed to remain focused on his task at hand and build his company. He was not interested in letting anyone eat his financial seed until he had cultivated it enough to sustain the needs of his personal household, his family, and his business. Once he felt he had secured a sustainable income stream, he created foundations that have given away far more than he ever could have given in the beginning of his career. He knew that by waiting until the right timing, he would be able to do more than a small quick fix. He carried the vision of the foundation within himself, stayed focused on working the plan, and brought it to fulfillment.

As women, we carry the CEO Code of finance within us and can create lasting impact if we move past the emotional pleas of those looking for our financial seed.

When we begin to look at community impact, there must be a plan that looks for areas where financial seed can grow, flourish, and multiply. Just throwing money at a community problem has never solved anything. Rather, an intentional, well-thought-out plan of action can turn the economic culture of a community. As women, we carry the CEO Code of finance within us and can create lasting impact if we move past the emotional pleas of those looking for our financial seed. We must become savvy in our planting so that we, and those in our lineage, can reap a harvest.

Uncovering your financial CEO DNA Codes will result in sustainability for your future, while investing into the lives of your community. Now that we have learned about all four codes, we can turn our attention to becoming wise and wealthy women.

Ask Yourself...

1. What financial perceptions do you carry regarding financial responsibilities within the home and your work environment?

2. Are you comfortable handling finances? Why or why not?

3. How do you handle financial setbacks?

4. Are you able to control your emotions during a financial discussion?

5. Do you believe that you are entitled to shortcuts and that the rules of finance do not apply in your situation?

6. What is the purpose for a job?

7. Please explain the difference between an asset and a liability.

8. How many streams of income flow into your home?

9. Can you name two additional untapped potential streams?

10. Do you believe that the CEO DNA Codes of creating wealth are already within you?

Section II:

Implementing
the CEO DNA Codes

Create a Plan of Action

Here is the key: women can intellectually understand that they carry the CEO DNA Codes within them. They can even agree that they are multidimensional and possess a variety of "giftings." But it is not until they create a ***plan of action*** for their individual lives that they can become fully functional in unlocking the codes that have been planted within them.

Chapter 7

Wise and Wealthy Women

I was impressed as I walked through the office, surveying my team as they worked. Each one was diligently working on the tasks at hand. I called for their attention to begin our weekly update regarding the progress of the business. I used this time to also reiterate our vision for the months, and year, to come. We had become a well-oiled machine, functioning as one, with our eyes on a common goal.

We caught up on the week's events, discussed new strategies and tactical implementations, and then settled back into our routines. Each team member understood her individual role, and each was blossoming personally and professionally. I sighed with contentment, aware of the importance and value of the team positioned around me.

Lunchtime came and I found myself sitting with one of our younger team members. She was smart, beautiful, and full of life. Her smile was contagious, continuous, and she performed at the speed of light! I always looked forward to the times when we could sit together and brainstorm ideas for upcoming events. But today something was wrong; things were *off*.

I knew I had a choice. I could sit and discuss business operations or goal development. I could answer work-related questions for her, or otherwise be "productive." Or, I could value the woman that sat just a few feet away from me and invest in her as an individual. I knew when I had hired her that she was essentially "on loan" to me and that one day she would leave to flourish in her own business. Until then, my responsibility was to pour into her life, mentor her, help her discover her CEO DNA Codes, and cultivate her skill sets. My goal was for her to be fully equipped to do what she had been created to do, perhaps doing greater things than I have ever done. She was being groomed to advance from my office as a successful, well-connected, confident woman, ready to take possession of her own territory within the business realm.

So, as she sat across from me, uncommonly nervous, biting her lower lip as she struggled to maintain composure, I intentionally laid down my papers and stepped across the line from a business owner to a character cultivator, purposefully seeking to help her.

It didn't take much. In fact, it was just a sentence or two before the tears began to trickle, randomly at first, and then gaining momentum as her story unfolded. She came from a broken home, had seen her mother abandoned, and had watched as family roles, responsibilities, and relationships had become blurred and then redefined. In her effort to help her mom, she had lost herself along the way. She assumed roles that had never been hers to play, and, in the process, laid down her own true callings for immediate responsibilities and requirements of life.

Working as part of the Crystal Clear Finances Team she saw the daily implementation of CEO DNA Codes in the women around her. This had awakened the desires within her for more. The hunger for self-fulfillment and purpose were fighting their way to the surface, fueled by the memories and dreams of her childhood. However, the "what if" and "shoulda, coulda, woulda" possibilities had begun to dominate her mind, causing her to focus on missed opportunities. She seemed stuck, aware of what was wrong, desiring what was right, but hopelessly struggling in a place of overwhelming confusion. She was desperately trying to gain traction regarding her true identity.

She had participated with the team as we used the CEO DNA Codes within us to set business administration goals. She had watched as we implemented our tactical operations by breaking our goals into manageable steps. Then, week-by-week, she was targeting and completing each one in order of priority. She had come to believe that a business built upon integrity could be successful. She was convinced that ethics and integrity would pay, and that as a team, we could take territory and have influence in the business realm. But she still faced the questions in her heart. These questions haunted her at night:

- Could the principles of a successfully woman-run business work for something other than a team of women? Could they be applied as effectively on a personal, solo basis?
- Could she, as a single woman, reap these same benefits?
- Did she have the right to believe that the CEO DNA Codes that she saw operating in the office could actually apply to her, as an individual woman? If so, did she have the right to claim them for herself?
- And, if so, how would she activate them in her own life?

I was stunned that one of my own team members would be struggling with such issues. After all, she had been working with us for a while and she saw practical applications of how to unlock a woman's CEO DNA Codes on a daily basis.

And yet through her hiccups, runny nose, and puffy eyes, she whispered her perceived sentence of death: "I don't know how...I see it right at my fingertips. It is so close that I can almost taste it. I dream about being confident in my womanhood, accomplishing what I dreamed of as a little girl. Yet those dreams are eclipsed by nightmares that taunt me, mocking me for believing that I could have any real destiny in this world. I am tormented for daring to believe that I personally could carry within me these CEO DNA Codes you talk about. I am at a point where I must either learn how to embrace what you have been teaching so I can silence the voices of condemnation and doubt, or let the CEO DNA seeds within me lay forever dormant."

Somehow we have been deceived into believing that success and the realization of all that was specifically designed for our lives is for the woman next door—never for us.

I realized that she was not an isolated instance, but a representative of a vast group of young women across this country who were battling these same issues on a daily basis. Somehow we have been deceived into believing that success and the realization of all that was specifically designed for our lives is for the woman next door—never for us. It is perceived and therefore believed that our individual fulfillment is unachievable; an elusive chase of an fleeting dream; that we will never embrace our womanhood and the seeds of greatness that are within.

Women read leadership books, go to seminars, attend self-help classes, and yet it still seems to elude them. They are in continual search of what they must DO in order to BE what they were called and equipped for in life.

A Plan of Action Is Needed

But here is the key: women can intellectually understand that they carry the CEO DNA Codes within them, they can even agree that they are multidimensional and possess a variety of giftings, but it is not until they create a plan of action for their individual lives that they can become fully functional in unlocking the codes that have been implanted within them.

We have all heard inspiring stories of women who were born into poverty and/or abuse only to overcome their circumstances to win, and win big. These determined individuals faced the world as underdogs and didn't give up until they realized their dreams. Their stories, places, and situations vary, but when you pull back the metaphors, mirrors, and makeup and investigate the fine details of their lives, you will notice a common thread that runs through each of these rags-to-riches fairy tales. The critical shift that brought breakthrough in their lives happened when they took the time to go back to their roots, when they searched for themselves and found their identity within themselves. That is when they broke out of their limitations and achieved greatness and significance. They intuitively discovered their CEO DNA Codes and activated them.

For those of us enjoying their biographies, reading their books, or seeing their dramas portrayed, the steps they needed to take were obvious. As we evaluate their lives from afar, we can recognize how their special idiosyncrasies could make them both happy and wealthy. All they needed to do was to go to their roots, accept their value, and then invest in cultivating themselves.

The answer is so obvious, and yet the lives on the screen or in print often report years of heartache before they reach that essential turning point, before they stumble upon the truth of simply appreciating and cultivating who they were. The same can be said regarding the women of today. We need to stop chasing the dreams and demands of others if we are to pay attention to ourselves. Otherwise, we will be overlooked in life's unending game of hide and seek.

**Sometimes, simplicity is
the ultimate sophistication!**

We often may find ourselves trapped in the game of life, constantly looking for someone else to define our roles and tell us who we are. We spend millions in counseling, therapy, self-help materials, and motivational seminars, searching vainly for the key that someone else has to unlock our inner selves. Women develop dependency relationships with others who dominate, intimidate, and manipulate them, just to feel secure in who the other person believes them to be. The simple step of slowing down and discovering the person we are seems too easy, and so we search for a different answer. Yet, sometimes, simplicity is the ultimate sophistication!

We have discussed in previous chapters the importance of understanding that women, as well as men, have a right to excel in this world. We were created with excellence built into the fabric of our being. In fact, not only do we have the right, but we also have the tools ingrained within us to succeed. It is now time to take these tools and bring their practical application to your life...today!

Please Step on the Scale

However, in order to start, you will have to endure five of the most hated words that a woman can hear: "Please step on the scale!"

I remember the first time I went to Weight Watchers™ and they asked me to step on the scale. There was a line of women behind me and beside me. There was no curtain, no private area, just a black square on the floor in front of me. I actually told the assistant that I already knew I was overweight, so there was no real reason for me to step on the scale and embarrass myself. It certainly wasn't going to tell me anything that I didn't already know. After all, I was here for a specific reason: to lose weight!

She was not amused, and once again repeated those offensive words in a slightly louder tone. She went on to explain that stepping on the scale wasn't a form of punishment or ridicule. Despite how it was making me feel, stepping on that scale was a starting point that would allow me to chart and then celebrate victories. If I was unaware of the extent of my weight, and the beginning of my journey, how would I ever be able to identify the milestones and celebrate victories along the way?

If you desire to awaken the CEO DNA Codes within you, then you too must "step on the scale" and evaluate how deeply they are buried. You must uncover those CEO DNA Codes hiding within.

Use Your Administration DNA Code to See the Big Picture

The CEO DNA Code of administration empowers women with the ability to see the big picture. It requires that you take the time to define your personal mission statement! Too many times we are so busy "living life," checking off the boxes on our "to do" list, that we do not live life with purpose. Break this cycle by taking some quiet time on a regular basis to listen to the messages that are within you, to cultivate your inner and almost infinite creativity. Being quiet positions you to receive inspiration.

Solitude or "quiet time" gives you the opportunity to think. We live in a world filled with so much stimulation, information, and entertainment that we seldom pull away to think. To paraphrase the Vietnamese monk, author, and peace activist, Thich Nhat Hanh:

If we are too busy, if we are carried away every day by our projects, our uncertainty, our craving, how can we have the time to stop and look deeply into the situation—our own situation, the situation of our beloved one, the situation of our family and of our community, and the situation of our nation and of the other nations?

I often sit by my pond with a hot cup of coffee and listen to the water run over the rocks. That is one of my places of refuge. Somehow the belching frogs and warring dragon-flies bring life back into perspective for me. I have found it to be a place of refueling. When life has been challenging or things begin to grow fuzzy, I head to the pond to putter with the flowers and watch the water ripple. Pretty soon tears that needed to be cried are dried and mountains go back to their molehills and life seems "doable" again.

We all need time for solitude in set-apart places to culti-vate our dreams, refresh our spirits, and plan for the future. In these places of peace and contentment, dream seeds are deposited and hope is watered. Don't be discouraged if you can't seem to dream or create a vision statement for your life. Be diligent to expose yourself to an atmosphere that is conducive for reflection and focus on just three areas of your life that you want to improve, change, or celebrate.

Once you have identified the three areas of life you want to improve, and you are ready to pay the price to be real, take a piece of paper and draw a line down the middle. On one side of the paper begin to write your strengths. Describe the gifts and talents you possess and the areas of work in which you find satisfaction. If money was no object and you didn't need a paycheck, what would you be doing? What areas would you focus on?

Be diligent to expose yourself to an atmosphere that is conducive for reflection and focus on just three areas of your life that you want to improve, change, or celebrate.

As you are creating the list of those areas in which you excel, activities that make you smile, or experiences that you want to pursue, write without hesitation or limitation. If you find it helpful, you can refer to the dream-building process in Chapter Three. Just remember that in this stage, you are simply seeking to know and acknowledge your strengths along with activities you would like to explore.

Now I know for many women, this may sound much easier than it really is. Unfortunately it is much harder than it should be. We have learned how to be quick in crucifying ourselves and slow to receive praise or validation. But a healthy perspective of our talents, strengths, and desires is needed in order to create a meaningful plan of action.

When you have finished the above, on the other side of the page begin to write what bothers you regarding your current situation. List the areas you struggle with, fears that continue to trip you up, and obstacles that you just can't seem to move past. You may not have to dig too deep for this list, as it seems this part of life tends to get more attention than it deserves.

I remember a season in my life not long ago when my world flipped upside down. I went from happy housewife, business owner, and public speaker, with the perception of owning the world, to facing an empty nest with all three of my children leaving home and a husband whose business now required him to travel. He was home only two days a month. Life became lonely and I shifted to survival mode. I didn't know how to dream or excel in this type of environment. Yet, I forced myself to believe that there was more that I could do than just survive—I could thrive!

As I sat on my rock by the pond and with the humming-birds flitting about, I watched as my tears and my dreams began to take form on my paper. I drew a line down the middle and on one side I identified what I loved in and about my life, as well as the strengths I felt I possessed. Although they seemed few, they were a glimmer of hope, serving to remind me that regardless of the situations around me, I still contained the CEO DNA Codes within me. I still had what was needed to push forward.

**As women, we need to know if the issues
we face are as bad as we think,
or are the harassments and obstacles
merely giants in our imaginations?**

On the other side of the paper, I wrote down the discouraging situations that overwhelmed me and the obstacles that appeared insurmountable. I identified every fear, whether fact or fiction, and put it on paper. I wanted to see them in black and white so I could evaluate what I was truly up against. It was time for these hindrances to step on the proverbial scale to see where they would weigh in.

As women, we need to know if the issues we face are as bad as we think, or are the harassments and obstacles merely giants in our imaginations? Those perceptions that are mental must be identified as such and crossed off the list. They are not real threats from the outside. These are internal, self-sabotaging illusions that keep many women prisoners. We must decide that we will not be our own worst enemy. Do not keep the war internal; take the battle external where it belongs.

The process of walking through life's trials and tests develops patience and perseverance, which produce character and self-confidence in the ability to cope effectively with the surprises of life.

Writing down my perceived weaknesses helped me realize that some were mere emotional misperceptions rather than facts. Those that had concrete and tangible validity could be dealt with by creating a plan. The process of walking through life's trials and tests develops patience and perseverance, which produce character and self-confidence in the ability to cope effectively with the surprises of life. This is essential to creating the customized plans of administrative processes necessary for true prosperity.

Albert Ellis' "Irrational Beliefs" provides thought-provoking insight to help challenge the thoughts that women unwittingly use against themselves. The key is to eliminate the lies that keep us unhappy, and prevent us from implementing the strategic plans needed to move forward.

Albert Ellis' "Irrational Beliefs" (Paraphrased)

- I need the love and approval of every significant person in my life.
- I must be competent and adequate in all possible respects.
- People (including me) who do things that I disapprove of are bad people who deserve to be severely blamed and punished.
- It's catastrophic when things are not the way I'd like them to be.
- My unhappiness is externally caused; I can't help feeling and acting as I do, and I can't change my feelings or actions.
- When something seems dangerous or about to go wrong, I must constantly worry about it.
- It is better for me to avoid than to face life's frustrations and difficulties.
- I need to depend on someone or something that is stronger than I am.
- Given my childhood experiences and the past I have had, I can't help being as I am today and I'll remain this way indefinitely.
- I can't help feeling upset about other people's problems.
- I can't settle for less than the right or perfect solution to my problem.2

Look over the above list. Think. Which of these irrational beliefs have infiltrated your mindset and have blocked your CEO DNA code? What steps will you take to change your thoughts, feelings, or actions in order to move beyond these mental blocks? Do you recognize that much of the battle to silence the CEO DNA Codes comes from within

---

2 Adapted from http://changingminds.org/explanations/belief/irrational_beliefs.htm

yourself? Women have learned to become their own worst enemy and unnecessarily keep themselves constrained within their own traps of condemnation and mental anguish.

However, this does not have to continue. Women, you have a choice; there is hope! Hope is the confident assurance that rises from within you and provides a platform of faith that empowers you to make significant and positive progress. With all that you have written, cried, tried and pushed through, begin to think of the places your skill sets can take you. Reflect on these important questions:

- What avenues do you wish to pursue and where are there open doors for you to go through?
- If all the threats that you described above were eliminated and you had clear sailing to pursue any avenue, where do you see yourself going?
- Do you know people who are there right now? Can they mentor you or give you advice?
- Are there open doors for schooling and advancement? Some places of employment offer tests that provide open doors to new levels.
- Are you assessing every situation around you to determine the opportunities that are hidden within?

The process you just experienced is formally called a SWOT analysis. It is an evaluation of the <u>S</u>trengths (codes), <u>W</u>eaknesses, <u>O</u>pportunities, and <u>T</u>hreats that are within and around you.

In terms of our strengths, we are often blind to our own life-changing skill sets and abilities, so we stumble unfulfilled though life like the underdogs we see portrayed on the movie screen. But today is your day to awaken and discover the CEO that is in Y-O-U! You have been endowed with all that is needed to bring you to the next level in your life. The codes are within you and simply need to be cultivated.

Use Your Operations DNA Codes to Set Up Your Goals

When you look back at your SWOT analysis, you can see there are areas of strengths, weaknesses, opportunities, and threats. It is critical that you take this list and identify the areas of strengths and opportunities that you wish to cultivate. Then outline a plan to bring it into maturity. Many times the end goal requires an upfront investment of time, resources, and diligence. It is up to you to determine how fully you wish to walk in the CEO DNA Codes that are ingrained within you. They will grow if you will consistently cultivate them.

Identifying the weaknesses and threats in your SWOT analysis is equally important. This will allow you to find the trigger gates in your life so you can intentionally close and seal them forever. Start with one area and find the root of what threatens you or is a perceived weakness. Pull up the root and get rid of its fruit!

Many individuals don't enjoy goal setting because they have tried before and "failed."

Many individuals don't enjoy goal setting because they have tried before and "failed." My advice is to start with the goals that are realistic and that you are willing to invest your time and effort in seeing achieved. Then determine what is needed each month, each week, and each day, and write out a plan of accomplishment.

In my earlier days, I remember that I was unhappy with my weight, so I would write down on my goal list that I wanted to drop thirty pounds and several dress sizes. Yet when I came to the steps of "operations" which required action steps and goal setting, I realized I would have to give up chocolate and make a major shift in my eating habits. At that point, I really wasn't ready to give up my treats, so I crossed it off my list. Chocolate was still *King* in my life! Several years later, I was tired of complaining about how unhealthy I felt and reevaluated the sacrifice it would take to get in shape. The focus had turned from a wishful "Barbie wannabe" to being a healthy woman. I was ready for the life change, and so I set and implemented the goal.

You are the one with the power to shift your life from the land of "wannabe" to "gonnabe." It will require work and attention to the plan that you establish, but it can...and must...be done!

Use Your Marketing DNA Codes to Be Yourself

The codes of sales/marketing require that you begin to take ownership of who you are and stop handing the rights and results of your life over to someone else. It is your life, and you must begin to believe and step out for yourself, because no one else can or will. What you present about yourself on a daily basis to your family, your friends, and your community is important. The message you give will either enforce your authority or it will self-sabotage your effectiveness.

As I mentioned in the marketing chapter, a message is constantly emitting from you. My question to you is, what do you want it to say? You are a living commercial. If you have started to cultivate your administration and operations CEO DNA Codes, then you are on your way to defining a mission statement for your life, or at minimum have specific personal goals.

Your personal marketing is how you are presenting yourself in relation to your goals. If you have set a goal for continuing education so that you can have the skill set for a better work environment or starting your own business, then the CEO DNA marketing that would align with this goal should include how you posture yourself, your overall grooming, disposition, and interaction with others. You will need to train yourself to be ready at all times for the door of opportunity to open. If you are diligently working your plan, then marketing is the outward manifestation of the inward change, and the indicator of the direction in which you are moving. How you speak shows hope or despair. How you dress can imply that you value yourself or that you see no value. Is your posture or demeanor one of desperation, or do you walk with confidence that all things will work together for your good?

If you are diligently working your plan, then marketing is the outward manifestation of the inward change, and the indicator of the direction in which you are moving.

Let me ask you, "Would you hire you?" If you heard that someone was trying to accomplish the goals that you have written down and they acted like you, dressed like you, talked like you, had the same friends as you, what would your reaction be to that person?

How we present ourselves to those around us is critical. You are marketing your success. This doesn't mean you are a phony and can never have a bad day. It does mean that you must have the inward strength and conviction to believe that you can accomplish every goal you have written down.

Use Your Finance DNA Codes to Create Wealth

Gone are the days of the white knights who ride in to take away all our financial problems. We can't hide at home and vacuum with pearls on. Finances are the currency we use to create business and meet our needs. Those who choose to be skilled in this area will reap a harvest.

As women, we must increase our financial literacy. We can read books, go to seminars, and study online; the avenues for growth are endless. We don't have to become Certified Financial Planners™, but we must understand the core basics of financial planning that are listed in Chapter Six.

I encourage you not to wait for a white knight to come, but rather learn to stand on your own. Find fulfillment in your ability to embrace your finances and to create a plan that will bring forth the resources needed to expand your influence! Your multiple streams of income can be managed so that the surplus is invested in assets that create more residual wealth. Take control of your finances! You can do it!!

Ask Yourself...

1. Are you letting your current situation dictate where you are headed?

2. Are you looking for others to define who you are and the role that you will embrace?

3. Are you ready to address the areas of life that you continually trip over?

4. What irrational beliefs are hindering you from embracing the CEO DNA Codes that you have within?

5. Complete a SWOT analysis and celebrate your strengths!

Motherhood

Let me assure you that true motherhood is not simply about feeding and clothing children until they reach adulthood, but rather it is an intentional focus on understanding and then strategically developing each child.

Chapter 8

"Mother, May I?"

"**I** hate you!"

I threw the Bible across the room and watched with great satisfaction as it hit the wall and collapsed to the floor in a crumpled mess. I didn't care. So what if the pages got crinkled or better yet; if they got ripped. I wasn't ever going to read it again anyways. Life wasn't fair, and I viewed God as a liar.

As I sat on the edge of my bed trembling with anger, I thought back to the time when I was five years old and first started to believe that there was a God. It was late and I had already been tucked into bed. Yet, between the doorbell and the storm that encouraged some branches to tap eerily against my window, I had awakened from my sleep. I was scared.

I heard my mom go to the door, so I slid out of bed, crept down the hallway, and sat unnoticed at the top of the stairwell. It was a safe place to listen; I could clearly hear the voices drifting up from the living room.

As I sat listening with my chin on my knees and my arms wrapped around my legs, I recognized that the voice belonged to the pastor down the road. His voice was nice and not mean like some of the preachers I had heard on television. I liked him.

I didn't understand everything they were talking about, but I was quite sure Mom was crying, although I didn't know why. The pastor was talking about a nice man who got killed when they put Him on a tree and made his head bleed. I couldn't figure out what the man did wrong. The pastor said that all He did was to love us so much that He died for all the bad things we had done. I squirmed uncomfortably. I wasn't sure what being out of bed would mean in that regard. Would he have to die again for my new sin?

But then the pastor said the nice man, named Jesus, wasn't dead anymore because His Father's name was God, and He was so strong that He beat death up, and we could be safe and go to heaven and live there. Oh, I hoped my mom and dad would say "yes" and we could go there! Then I wouldn't have to be scared in my bed anymore.

It got quiet and they were whispering, so I snuck down a few steps and heard they were talking to Jesus. I don't know how He got in the room; maybe the pastor brought Him. Either way, they were telling Him they were sorry and they wanted to go to heaven. I wanted to go too. I stood up hesitantly. Do I go down and meet Jesus and tell Him that I want to go to heaven too, or could I just tell Him here on the stairs? I heard them say "amen," and then I knew they were just praying and I could do that anywhere.

So, before they could catch me out of bed, I sat on the third step down from the top and asked Jesus to be my friend. I asked Him if I could go to His house for a sleepover some day and offered that He could come to mine—as long my mom said it was okay. I told Him I was sorry for all the bad things I had done and I would really try to be good, and I was even sorry for getting out of bed tonight.

When I was done, I wasn't scared anymore. I had a new friend. I went back to my room and even the branches didn't scare me anymore. I figured if Jesus' Dad could heal His Son from being dead, He could protect me too. From that point on, Jesus and I were BFFs—Best Friends Forever! In school and on the soccer field, during tests, and even when I was being picked on, I never doubted that He was there. I started reading the Bible when it was just pictures and grew to read consistently every day. I could tell Him anything and trust Him with everything.

Until today...

Only moments earlier I had returned home from the doctor's after receiving the news that my son would be born with severe mental handicaps. They had offered to abort him and erase the problem that this would inevitably cause my family. In essence, they had offered to make it "all go away."

I had felt justified that my exemplary behavior would qualify me to have perfectly-formed children with high intelligence and purposeful lives.

If I drank, smoked, and had taken drugs, I could justify why this was happening. Up to this point, I had naively assumed that those who had a child with any type of deformity or abnormality was somehow reaping what they had sown. In retrospect, that was such a terribly ignorant and ugly thought. Yet, I had felt justified that my exemplary behavior would qualify me to have perfectly-formed children with high intelligence and purposeful lives. After all, I hadn't broken any of the big rules; I hadn't committed any "big" sins!

And yet now, what good had it done? Although I would love my child, I could never protect him from the cruel insults of this world. They wouldn't take the time to really see my son, but would seek ways to alleviate the discomfort of his presence. I felt that there was nothing I could do to stop all of this from happening.

I got up and left the room, and for the next few weeks the crumpled Bible stayed in a heap, an outward manifestation of my inner frustration. I fought with myself continually as I fell into the old pattern of talking to Jesus like my friend instead of the uncaring person that I now believed Him to be. Finally I could stand it no more. I couldn't lose the baby within and lose my best friend too.

**Life is not about trying to be problem free.
Rather, it is working together and growing stronger
through each situation we face.**

When the house was quiet, the girls were sleeping, and George was off at work, I walked over to the Bible. I could feel life and death hanging in the balance. I stared motionless for what seemed hours, and then slowly I bent over and picked it up. One by one I smoothed out the pages, put the ripped sheets in proper order, and then closed my eyes and prayed: "God, I don't know why and I don't understand. But I have known You since I was five and You have always been with me. I don't know how to do anything else but love You. I am sorry for believing You had abandoned me in the midst of this overwhelming crisis. The Bible is either all truth or all a lie. I choose to believe You are true. Please help me through this."

During the next two months, I prepared for my son's arrival. Three days after Christmas, George V, our little king, was born! There were three doctors on call and as each one inspected my son, they shook their heads in amazement and pronounced him healthy. Once again God had been merciful…and faithful.

Many times we believe that because we are good people, good neighbors, or good parents, nothing bad can ever happen to us. We think we should be able to give birth to perfect children who will live with us as perfect parents in our perfect homes and enjoy perfect lives. We somehow have bought into the illusion that raising kids and being a fulfilled wife is about getting to a point where we have no problems or issues to deal with. Life is not about trying to be problem free. Rather, it is working together and growing stronger through each situation we face.

I have noticed that when women become mothers, they tie on the red cape and frantically pursue being a Super Mom. They have the illusion that if dinner is on the table at 6:00 p.m. when Dad comes home, the house is spotless, their kids are healthy and well behaved, and the neighbors like them, then everything should be fine.

They run ragged trying to meet invisible, ever-changing social expectations. And yet, despite the fact that they do all the right things, it just doesn't work, and the frustration of being robbed of their dream of perfection emerges. After all, moms are supposed to have well-adjusted, well-mannered children who understand the importance of presenting a strong family name. Additionally, they should have husbands who are supposed to stay up late listening to their concerns. Of course, they also expect to have a lifetime of courtship. Unfortunately, such families are either myths or rare exceptions and not the rule.

Good behavior only works for parole situations, not in the real world! Life is multidimensional, and although your influence will impact future generations, it does not guarantee a specific result. It only provides a solid foundation for the right choices to be implemented.

Therefore we must not assume that securing the titles of "wife" and "mom" entitles us to live happily ever after without the need to apply intentional or strategic effort. To the contrary, being a mom is an assignment of distinction that requires the complete activation of every CEO DNA Code within you!

Let me assure you that true motherhood is not simply about feeding and clothing children until they reach adulthood, but rather it is an intentional focus on understanding and then strategically developing each child.

The statement, "The hand that rocks the cradle rules the world," is not some flippant statement offered as a generic general pat on the back to placate those who are called to be mothers. Rather, it was a sober acknowledgement that the primary influencers of all human life are those who give guidance and correction to children during their most formative years. Most interpret the role of "mother" as requiring every mom to stay at home. That misunderstanding is commonly used to "guilt" women into compromising their own individual well-being and diminishing their own fulfillment. It is often used as a whip to condemn and criticize women who go into the workplace, implying that they are deserting their role as moms, and thereby betraying their children. Ironically, many of these working moms are providing important role models for their children by demonstrating what it means to pursue one's personal goals and achieve individual fulfillment.

Let me assure you that true motherhood is not simply about feeding and clothing children until they reach adulthood, but rather it is an intentional focus on understanding and then strategically developing each child.

Just because a woman is staying home during the day to be physically present for her children does not mean that her parenting is being done in an intentional manner. There are plenty of children who belong to stay-at-home moms who are being raised by televisions! So, in fairness to all women, we need to move past the limiting stereotyping of "motherhood" and start evaluating the quality of the parenting and the results thereof.

I had the privilege of being a stay-at-home mom until all my children were in school. Then I worked only during school hours while they were in middle school, and subsequently transitioned into full-time development of Crystal Clear Finances as they entered high school. So I am well aware of the challenges and benefits of both being at home and being in the business world.

Raising children is one of the few occupations that guarantee you permanent employment! You are a parent for life in the sense that your influence will significantly impact the course and growth of your child for the rest of his or her life.

Not all my children are the same, and neither are yours. That is why each one requires an individualized, customized life plan.

I remember some of the intentional training that I did with my oldest child, Melonie, when she was a young teenager and began working at my office. During one session we spent over thirty minutes of role-playing on how to answer the phone! Over and over I drilled her on the importance of smiling when she said hello, making sure there was no slang in any of her responses, always introducing herself, and asking how she could help the caller. She was neither impressed nor thankful for this training. In fact, during her teenage years, I very seldom made her list of top ten favorites. Yet, I knew that even as a young woman she had the

CEO DNA Codes within her, and my job was to help her cultivate them.

Not all my children are the same, and neither are yours. That is why each one requires an individualized, customized life plan. That may sound complex and overwhelming, but in actuality, it is relatively simple. It just requires time, thought, attention, and focus!

When my children were between the ages of three and seven, I brought home a storybook that was helpful in revealing their internal tendencies. It was a story of four friends who spent a day together. One of the friends always made the journey fun, suggesting things like roasting marshmallows, going sailing, or having a party. Another friend would take those ideas and make sure that all the supplies needed to make them happen were available. The third friend felt it was very important that someone be giving directions such as where the fire should go and how long it should last. He picked the sailboat and steered the ship. The last friend made sure everyone was okay. He didn't want to lead, come up with the idea, or prepare; he just wanted everything to stay calm and everyone to stay happy.

As I read these stories, we would stop after each adventure and I would ask the children who their favorite person was and why. My son George always liked the fact that there was going to be a party and thought of all the fun activities that they could do. His choice revealed to me that his natural tendencies would place him as the center of attention. He would thrive with people around him and move quickly from one idea to another. This also meant details, organization, and the like, were areas that would need to be brought to his attention. These would not be his strengths.

Melonie was more focused on the strategy and the administrative details needed to implement the ideas, as well as the leadership required to get the job done. She wanted to see the repercussions of every option before moving forward. She was extremely cautious. This provided the insight I needed to communicate effectively with her. She would need all the details up front, and then time to review them without pressure or time constraints. Even as an adult, I watch her make decisions that are carefully calculated, with little room for surprises. Her career path, which includes law school, is a perfect match for her internal skill set.

Stephanie, my middle child, would listen to the stories and identify what needed to be done in order for everyone to enjoy themselves. Even as a small child she would make a list so that nothing and no one would be overlooked. Her attention to detail has opened many doors for her to plan and host numerous events and weddings, each with hundreds of attendees. Today she is a premiere event planner and executive administrator in a prominent university, where she has impacted her environment through her ability to effectively implement all of her lists!

While both my daughters have commendable traits, they can also lose themselves in tasks and overlook the fun moments in life. The ability to embrace the unscheduled and sometimes the most meaningful moments of life needs to be cultivated to the same level as their task capabilities. That will all happen in time, but only because we will be intentional about it!

The above is just an example of one way to intentionally understand the natural tendencies of your children. This can help you to begin to developing their strengths and undergirding their weaknesses. This is no different than a CEO in the business realm understanding the strengths and weaknesses of the team members around her. It takes the same skill set as performing "due diligence" on a company with whom they may be partnering, and it is the same capability required to manage a project being brought from vision to reality. Yet sometimes, as women, we leave the above skill sets and our executive savvy at the front door and use our "mom" title as a way to downplay our responsibility. "What's for dinner?" is sometimes given more attention than nurturing the stagnating DNA Codes within our children.

As a woman you must come to a place where you know your strengths, and areas for growth, and have a plan for your life. You must also know your family and have a plan for each of them as well.

It is easy to adopt a defensive attitude and claim that your children won't allow you to sow into their lives, but that is where leadership comes in. In the previous chapters we have dealt with the issues that plague women and add to their insecurities. As a woman you must come to a place where you know your strengths, and areas for growth, and have a plan for your life. You must also know your family and have a plan for each of them as well. Having your own intentional plan of growth is a prerequisite for creating one for your children and your marriage. After all, you can't send people where you, yourself, have never been. Model the behavior that you desire to attract and you will awaken it within them.

I once heard John Maxwell talk about the Five "Ps" of leadership, as noted below. Leadership does not just exist in the workplace. As an individual, it must first start within your own personal life and your home...only then can it move forward.

Position. On Level One, the key word is Position. Your influence and authority in the home is based solely upon your title as "mom" and the position you hold as such. Following your commands is not optional, and so your children submit and do as they are told. At least that is how it is supposed to work! Although they need to recognize that you are the authority in the house, leading by dictatorship is seldom fulfilling for anyone involved.

Permission. Level Two is when you lead through Permission, where those who are being led obey out of their love and respect for you. It is a servant leader culture where the key word is relationship. While this does not imply that you are a servant to your children, it is a recognition that they do not exist to serve you. In this arena, it is best to cultivate an atmosphere where there is still position of respect from which to govern.

Production. Level Three in leadership is defined by Production. You have successfully conveyed the goals that you are seeking to achieve within each individual and as a family. When my daughter Stephanie was in high school, she had the opportunity to travel to Africa with her father to build an orphanage. Her brother George had the same opportunity. Yet, Stephanie knew this was her last year of living at home and asked her brother if he would stay behind on this trip to give her some special alone time with her father. George knew this trip had been one of Stephanie's key goals, and so he stepped aside so Stephanie could travel alone with her father. And, as a family unit we worked together to help earn the funds so she could go.

**Respect for us as women
cannot be demanded; it must be earned.**

People. Level Four is displayed through People. At this point the family unit has realized that it is not just about one person and their needs. It is a team effort, and people development is valued. We have learned that the well-being of one contributes to the well-being of all.

Pinnacle. Level Five is the Pinnacle. At this point the relationship with your team or family has been established, unity has been cultivated, and the family follows because of who you are and the integrity you represent. It has nothing to do with your leadership title of "mom," but has everything to do with respect. Unfortunately, many moms try to demand this level of leadership without taking the intentional steps to cultivate a team atmosphere. Respect for us as women cannot be demanded; it must be earned. This is yet another reason why women need to first address their own strengths and weaknesses, and define their own intentional path of growth.

The strength of character of each woman will be tested and stretched as they enter the realm of motherhood, of that you can be sure!

I encourage you to take a moment and look through the list of Five "Ps," above, and determine where you believe your leadership influence stands as of today. Once you know your starting point, you can work intentionally to increase your influence.

It is time that as mothers, we recognize that regardless of whether we spend the majority of our time working outside of the home or within it, we must take our job seriously and apply every skill set we have.

The children you were given to raise were not by accident. Fortunately, long before you were given those children you were also given the skill sets needed to accomplish your parental tasks. Yet, that is just the starting point! It is a foundation that you can build upon to develop yourself and intentionally cultivate your children and the destinies within them.

Be aware, there will be times that you can do everything correctly and your children may turn and walk away. They do not see the value of your consistency and your training. It is like the Charlie Brown cartoon where the teacher's voice drones on and on with no one understanding what is being said. There will be times when your children haven't a clue as to what you are doing or why!

Being intentional regarding your children does not guarantee perfect results, but what it does allow is a culture and atmosphere for growth to happen. You can't control their emotions or thoughts, and as they get older, and you can't control many of their actions. But you can control your own thoughts, emotions, and actions, resulting in consistent training, consistent influence, and nurturing culture.

Throw away the unrealistic self-satisfying illusions of what you feel your children should be and instead discover who your child is.

Throw away the unrealistic self-satisfying illusions of what you feel your children should be and instead discover who your child is. Then do everything in your influence to create the connections and training needed to help them excel.

We Must Use the CEO Finance Codes at Home!

As mentioned earlier, during the time when my children were all under the age of five, we were in a season where finances were extremely limited. My full-time job was raising three children, and George's trucking company lost their largest customer. We had just purchased a home and drained our accounts in order to meet the down payment. This event triggered a downward spiral that took seven years to recover from. During that time, we had many nights without electricity and we learned to heat with wood. Food was minimal and the luxury of cookies was simply not an option. We explained the situation to the children the best that we could and kept pointing to the hope that someday we would have a surplus and this would only be a memory.

At the end of our fourth year, we were beginning to get some traction and we found ourselves with an extra ten dollars for the week. We were headed home from an event and the kids were complaining that they were hungry. Little George began to whine for McDonald's. As we were getting closer to the turns that would take us either to the grocery store or to McDonald's, Melonie turned to him and said, "Bubby, quit whining. We have ten dollars to spend. We can either go to McDonald's to fill your stomach for tonight, or we can go to the store and buy bread, peanut butter, and some apples and eat for a week. Stop thinking about just what you want for today!" It was then I realized that she had grasped the concept between needs versus wants. She had realized that finances needed accountability in how they were spent.

Understanding the CEO DNA codes of administration, operations, sales/marketing, and finance WILL help you intentionally raise a family.

Many times we feel guilty for not investing more time with our kids so we give them free reign in the area of finances. We spend on their wants and rob them of the opportunity to experience delayed gratification and self-denial.

We need to understand that despite what our kids think, WORK is not a four-letter word! Work can be one of the most effective tools for character development and fiscal responsibility. Helping our children understand, that just because there is money in the bank and you can afford it, doesn't mean it needs to be spent. "No" is an acceptable answer!

Understanding the CEO DNA codes of administration, operations, sales/marketing, and finance WILL help you intentionally raise a family. You can administrate and understand the vision for your children, use operations to create a plan for helping them reach their goals, implement sales/marketing to create an atmosphere for them to grow, and teach finance through fiscal responsibility. Remember, you are their parent, not their peer. Develop and provide opportunities, but put the "red cape" away and don't force results! Above all, remember—it's never too late to intentionally love your child!

Ask Yourself...

1. Do you struggle with the perception of being the perfect mom?

2. Is your self-worth and validation tied to the success and performance of your children?

3. What steps are you taking to intentionally train your children?

4. Are you looking to become your child's peer buddy or his or her mom? What is the difference?

5. Do you want your daughter to carry the same perceptions regarding her role as a woman that you do?

6. What level of leadership describes your role as mom in the home?

The Code of Love

Unconditional love refuses to cut a partner loose, but rather works to bring them successfully through the growth process. It is a skillful game of advancement where personal growth in each spouse is required and then supported in a team atmosphere. It is very similar to the unity and mutual dependence required to win in a three-legged race.

Chapter 9

Marriage Master

I was thirteen when I met George. When I was eighteen, we were married and I assumed we would live happily ever after. After all, why shouldn't we? We were in love!

No one ever told me that being a wife would require effort! I didn't realize that I would need to intentionally activate every CEO DNA Code within me. Looking back, I wish someone had given me the following insights. Life would have been so much easier!

My Top Ten Tips for Marriage

1. *Watch Your Words!* Being quick with the tongue can be fun when you are verbally sparring with a friend, but when words become ugly and cut deep, it's time to close your mouth! As my friend, Irene, says: "Just because it comes into your mind doesn't mean it needs to come out of your mouth!" As a wife and mother this is critical, because saying you're sorry after you have verbally degraded your spouse or child does not heal all of the wounds. I remember one time when I was fighting with George and I verbally described every fault

I saw in him. After the fight was over, I went on my merry way. That night when I snuggled up to him and told him how great he was, he softly answered, "How can I be so wonderful when just hours ago I was a complete failure? I have done nothing different since this afternoon. So what changed?" It was at that moment we came to an agreement that personal verbal attacks would not be allowed.

2. *Get a Room!* That is one of the most repeated phrases that my children tell me. Displays of affection, done with good taste and proper boundaries, can provide a sense of comfort to your children and edify your spouse in the process. It is important for your children to know, again and again, where your affections lie, so that when there are those inevitable disagreements, they know you and your spouse are still committed to each other. An unfortunate number of children grow up in households where words of affection and proper physical touching between parents are missing. And children miss the nurturing words and loving touch from their parents when they are not provided. Though they jest and declare a kiss from Mom (or Dad) is "gross," it is usually a statement of, "Stop it! Stop it! I love it!"

3. *And the Answer is....* Before my children were born, I would ride with George in his tractor trailer and spend days on the road with him as he delivered his various loads. I would bring along a book called *The Question Book* that held page after page of questions like: "If your house was on fire and your children and spouse were safe, what three items would you retrieve and why?" That question would trigger memories and/or concerns and ultimately generate even more questions! Hours would pass as George and I shared stories and learned intricate

details about each other. So, take time to learn about your spouse. Look for opportunities, such as *The Question* book. It will provide clarity and insight as to why we react differently to the same situations. That understanding can create strong foundations for your marriage.

4. *Growth Spurts.* I met George when I was thirteen and married him at eighteen. I felt so grown up. Unfortunately my emotional maturity didn't match my age, and George spent the next seven years taking me from a spoiled little girl to a more mature woman who could be an effective life partner. As I matured, we stumbled across areas where George had some "opportunities" for growth. It was my turn to help him mature in those areas. This became a pattern where one of us would make an advance in our personal growth and then help the other to come alongside.

Unfortunately, our culture does not encourage that pattern. It tends to encourage the partner who has advanced in his or her development to cut ties with their marriage partner, and leave that old "dead weight" partner, while they search for another partner. This is highly destructive.

The whole growth process involves the discovery of limitations and immaturity in our lives. We need to give ourselves permission to see these problems for what they are and then work through them with the help of our spouse and other family members. No couple ever grows in the same way, in the same areas or in the same timeframe. Growth is a game of leapfrog, where one runs ahead in a given area, then is jumped over by the other in some other area of growth. Unconditional love refuses to cut a partner loose, but rather works to bring them successfully through the growth process. It is a skillful game of advancement where personal growth in each spouse is required and then supported in a team atmosphere. It is very similar to the unity and mutual dependence required to win in a three-legged race.

5. *Lovin' It.* Have you ever met a woman who seems to have it all together? She isn't upset when you don't like her, or the way she dresses, how she looks, or where she works. She is at peace with herself and doesn't see the importance of having to prove herself to anyone. She doesn't fear rejection because she has already accepted herself. She operates from a position of stability and is not easily thrown off track. This stems from being at peace with who she is and being comfortable in her own skin.

   I remember reading yet another magazine that promised to show me how to be beautiful. I asked my husband what he thought made me beautiful. He said that it was my confidence; the ability to be at ease with myself.

   As wives, we need to realize that we are not in competition with airbrushed movie stars, and we do not have to measure up to the myths and irrational expectations of our unhappy society. We simply need to discover who we are and then celebrate ourselves and our many positive attributes. When we become comfortable in our own skin, and are at peace with who we are, then we can have some serious impact.

6. *In Other Words....* Have you ever had a conversation with a couple and one spouse did all the talking, even when you were addressing the other person? There was a time when I was so insecure about who I was that I needed everyone to approve of me, my marriage, and my family. This meant that my husband had to be perfect, or at least appear to be so. I felt that any mistake he made would be a reflection on me. I didn't want

him to do anything to embarrass me, which meant I lived on pins and needles! I assumed that the only way I could avoid any embarrassment would be to finish his sentences for him! I would squeeze his knee under the table so he knew when to talk and when to be silent. If he didn't get the signal to stop, I always had the ever-effective kick to jog his memory! None of this worked. The problem wasn't my husband, or what he said, or even the people who were listening, but the lie I had believed about needing approval from everyone in order to feel good about myself. Nothing would provide me with relief until I faced down that lie.

Manipulating, controlling, or muzzling your spouse or child is a big step down a slippery hill. Each person needs to express themselves freely, otherwise a power struggle will ultimately develop and threaten the relationship.

There must be an atmosphere of respect where each voice can be heard. This is more than just gritting your teeth and holding your breath while they talk. It is learning to relax and enjoy them as individuals. Give them space so they can grow!

Over-controlling is the act of an immature, insecure individual, one who needs to take a journey into the land of self-development for the sake of all inhabitants!

7. *Game Changer.* Every summer we put air conditioners in the windows around the house. We have three zones where we shut the doors and lock in the nice, cold air. As you walk from room to room, you can tell whose zone you are in. I don't need a sweatshirt in my area, but I am almost convinced that my son is trying to grow icicles in his room! I have learned to carry a sweater if I am going to spend any time in that section of the house!

As women, we have the unique ability to create an atmosphere of warmth and comfortable acceptance within our sphere of influence. Unfortunately, we also can turn a room into the North Pole with just one cold blast of our tongue! We must come to the place where we realize we are the ones who control our atmosphere. We are the ones who change the temperature. We create the environment that we are going to thrive or die within, so we must choose wisely. This not only applies to our home, but also to every place we inhabit.

8. *Ready, Set, Action!* Regardless of your inner intentions, it will be your actions and reactions that speak the loudest. As a wife and mother, you are a role model, and the rules and regulations and the pattern of daily living you establish within your home have a high probability of being duplicated in the lives and future homes of those who are watching. When wives allow themselves to be verbally mistreated by their husbands, their daughters usually grow up to marry a husband who will do the same. It isn't right, and it isn't healthy, but it is familiar. And so the destructive environment of one home becomes the norm for many homes. Over several generations, many are adversely affected. Those not directly involved in the situation can encourage the wife to stand up and challenge the inappropriate treatment, but to them it has become an ingrained normality. It will take a lot of effort to change. But change we can!

My son often brings his friends over to the house. My husband and I enjoy interacting with them and as I mentioned before, we have been affectionately named Mama and Papa Bear. The other day one of the young "cubs" made the comment that he hated his father. When we dug deeper, he began to relay many instances of his father's poor behavior. In his eyes, his father had betrayed not only him, but the whole family. He was confused and distraught over his father's disregard for the family. The good news is that this "cub" was sorting through his own thoughts as to what was right, what was wrong, and how he was going to live his life. He was not going to allow the misconduct of his father to unhinge his life. That is mature thinking for such a young man!

We may not think our kids are watching, but they are observing everything we say and do, and unless strong, positive foundations are put in place, they will be in jeopardy to repeat our dysfunctional patterns.

9. *Goal Setting.* The other day my husband was in the area and asked if I would like to take a short trip in his truck. I thought this would be a great opportunity to bond even more, so I quickly answered, "Yes." I assumed a short trip would mean something around one to two hours. However, I found out that his idea of a short trip and my idea differ by about eight to ten hours! Yet, his excitement that I was coming with him to get an understanding of his world was worth every minute that I spent bouncing around in the passenger seat of that huge truck.

Too many times husbands and wives are off pursuing their own areas of interest and they lose the common ground they once shared. I have found that it is key to not only visit the areas of interest that your spouse may have, but also to discover and cultivate those areas and activities that can be enjoyed together. Memories are powerful weapons to maintain unity when times get tough. Intentionally creating memories and finding areas of unity provide a safeguard for the future.

Every year George and I share our individual goals with each other, but we also create goals that include each other. These are not just "To Do" lists, but include fun items as well. Plan dates, cultivate interests, and continue the courtship! Propel one another into new levels of achievement.

10. *Never Quit.* During the course of the past twenty-six years of marriage, I have visited the edge of bankruptcy, seen a business dissolve, almost lost my home, and had negative balances in my checkbook. I have had children cry and spit up all over me, and had teenagers scream, yell, and drive off into the night. I have watched loved ones die, friends move away, relationships dissolve, and have often cried myself to sleep. I have faced losing my identity, my voice, and my way. If had given up, then I would have never seen new businesses grow and old businesses strengthened. I would have never seen my house transition into a real home, full of my own teenagers and their friends. I wouldn't have experienced the deeper relationships that come from true repentance and deep healing.

    Perhaps quitting and running from these situations could have provided temporary relief, but facing life matures your soul, develops your voice, clarifies your directions, and strengthens your understanding of who you are. Just as we honor and respect our veterans of war for valiantly fighting and holding firm for our freedom, we should reflect back on the battles we have endured and honor ourselves for the strength and perseverance we have shown. With that encouragement, we can face the future with a healthy respect for our ability to overcome whatever challenges life may bring. It is not always about "winning" or "losing," but about the ability to stand firm and persevere against all odds.

Change Can Be Good!

I have been blessed with a husband who is my best friend. As a business owner, he had reached a place where he dispatched his trucks from home. Every morning we had breakfast by the pond, complete with my favorite blueberry coffee. Dinner was ready when I walked in the door each night, and we enjoyed evenings swinging on the porch, recounting the events of the day!

Then one day, the phone rang and everything changed. His driver was in Ohio and was in the hospital with an appendicitis attack. George immediately became both the driver and dispatcher for his business. Gone were the days of breakfast, dinner, and time together. Soon he was home barely two days a month, and even then it was just enough time to wash clothes, process paperwork, and head back out the door.

As wives, we are sometimes faced with the realization that what could have been, may never be again.

While this was not the same as losing my spouse permanently, it was still a serious problem! Our lives experienced a 180-degree turnaround from our previous lifestyle of daily interaction. I was lost. I no longer had my bearing, and for months waffled between pitiful and pathetic! I couldn't remember how to function as an individual. Although it was a healthy marriage, I had lost my anchor.

Well-meaning friends encouraged me to find things I liked to do. The problem was, I couldn't remember what those were. It had been so long since I had been alone. I had been mother, businesswoman, and wife. It took months of sitting alone by the pond, reading books, writing my

SWOT analysis, and trying new things, before I learned that coming home to an empty house is okay. I can enjoy life as a woman, mother, and wife without my children or George being present.

As wives, we are sometimes faced with the realization that what could have been, may never be again. It is at these moments in life that we must realize that we are not victims and that we still have choices. We may not be able to change the actions, thoughts, or work patterns of our spouse, but we can control our own thoughts, actions, and outlook. At such times, we have the right and the responsibility to awaken the woman within and cultivate her so that she can live, and live abundantly, once again.

We do not have to be a picture-perfect Barbie with the best home on the block in order to be a good wife. We can relax in our role and approach it with the same intentional focus that we did when we embraced motherhood.

Using Administrative Codes at Home

Whether we are functioning in the role of mother or wife, the codes of Administration hidden within must be brought to the surface. These codes will allow you to cultivate a dream for your family and your marriage.

Women must take time to visualize the impact and scope of their legacy. In our household, I am actively cultivating a legacy of entrepreneurship and leadership, which includes the ability to strategize, and create positive team culture. What do you see as the defining DNA of your household? What are the personal dreams and goals for your household and your marriage? It is not enough to say that you don't like where things are headed. You must define where you want them to go and intentionally steer them in that direction.

Knowing the skill sets within yourself, your spouse, and each of your children can position you to confidently advance as a team. This takes diligent research as noted in the previous chapter, but is critical to ensure that you and your family can move forward, strategically advancing towards your goals. The more effective intelligence gathering is, the more significant your advance will be.

Create a plan to understand your spouse and your kids. You will need to know their skill sets, their love languages, methods of effective communication, and their pattern for processing information.

Create a plan to understand your spouse and your kids. You will need to know their skill sets, their love languages, methods of effective communication, and their pattern for processing information. Once you are armed with this information, the next step is implementation through the Code of operations.

Using the Operations Code in Your Family

In my home office I have a glass top the covers my desk. It keeps the top from being scratched and the desk looking pristine! Under the glass, on the left-hand side is an 8x10 piece of paper where my goals are listed for the year. There are five categories listed down the side:

- Personal
- Family & Spouse
- Financial
- Work
- Community

Every day as I sit at my desk, I review the goals and confirm my commitment to see them completed.

Yet, to just sit and promise myself that they will be completed without implementing a plan of action is hypocritical in nature. In order to be a woman of my word, I must take the steps needed.

As mothers and wives, we need to take the information we gathered during our administrative assessment and then day by day take action to enforce the plan. I have found it helpful to list what must be accomplished each month, break it down to weekly assignments, and then daily activities. Operations will help keep a progress chart of your advancement towards the goals.

Again, I want to emphasize that this is not about implementing "your" goals for your family, but rather setting goals that will help uncover their dreams and then assisting them in reaching those dreams. By the time they leave the home environment, they should have a successful track record of accomplishments that they can look back upon. This can provide extra encouragement during times when they are facing new situations and they are unsure of the outcome.

Put Sales/Marketing Codes to Work in Your Family

Establishing culture within a home is like determining the temperature at which a thermostat should be set. The right temperature is one that provides the most comfort and well-being for all who use the area. The right culture creates an atmosphere that inspires personal growth with the safety to fail.

My son has a friend who often comes over and stays up late watching movies with him. There have been many mornings where I have quietly tiptoed past him as he was asleep on the couch. Recently we noticed that he comes over even when our son isn't home. He grabs his pad of paper and heads to the couch to sketch. He is drawn to the atmosphere and has found a haven where he can relax and focus on developing his talent.

We have noticed this among other neighborhood young adults as well. Just the other night, George pulled in with his tractor trailer and everyone jumped up from the campfire and followed him into the kitchen to hear about his trip and swap stories. One by one as they had their fill, they drifted back out to the campfire, each leaving when their connection had been completed and their need for "Papa Bear" had been satisfied.

While many would not list this as marketing, creating a family culture and a safe environment where family and friends can really connect is critical. Marketing is the culture of legacy that you are creating in your home.

While many would not list this as marketing, creating a family culture and a safe environment where family and friends can really connect is critical. Marketing is the culture of legacy that you are creating in your home. It can be shown in a variety of different ways, from cleaning your home, to room design and furniture, to the food in the fridge, and the open door policy that you keep. Each decision builds upon another to help create the atmosphere that is key to the family DNA and purpose. It is a dream-conducive atmosphere of acceptance of not only who you are now, but also an understanding of where you intend to be!

Each family member hears love and acceptance in their own way. We can be living with the illusion that we are effectively displaying and conveying love to our family and spouse and yet completely miss the mark.

When George and I were first married, he used to follow me around the house while I was doing chores, trying to talk to me. It was so annoying! I would have really appreciated it if he would have stopped talking and helped me complete the tasks at hand. After all, I had a lot to do and he was getting in the way! Then one day we got into a discussion and I asked him if he could please not only tell me that he loved me, but also learn to show it by helping me. He looked at me in surprise and said he was constantly reaching out to me and trying to show me he loved me, but I kept pushing him way.

Once George and I identified our love languages, we were able to more effectively communication with one another.

I asked him what he was talking about, and to give me an example. He said, "Every day, I try to take time to come and sit with you so we can talk and you never make time for me. You just scurry from task to task and refuse to interact with me." Now it was my turn to be shocked. I never viewed his actions as an invitation to sit and talk; I saw his behavior as meaning that he didn't want to help me work!

After talking, we realized that sitting down and having time where I am not preoccupied or sharing my attention was important to him and was a way that I could effectively communicate my love. In return, he realized that picking up a rag to help dry the dishes or folding laundry with me was an effective way to communicate to me in my love language.

In the book, *The Five Love Languages,* by Gary Chapman, we found that there are five basic levels of communicating love and acceptance: Touch, Verbal Affirmation, Acts of Service, Quality Time, and Gift Giving. Once George and I identified our love languages, we were able to more effectively communication with one another.

Ask Yourself...

1. Have you ever felt betrayed? How did you resolve it?

2. Are you setting unrealistic expectations for yourself?

3. Have you identified and established boundaries that will keep you from physically and emotionally burning out?

4. Do you allow the reaction of others to define your worth? Why?

5. Do you take time to celebrate and nurture yourself?

6. What are your "Top Ten Tips for Marriage?"

Be Productive, Not Busy

Too many business owners take pride in how busy they are. They do not understand that **activity is not the same as progress**. Frantic efforts do not always result in more business, improved revenues, or better cash flow. Those owners are often more satisfied with the illusion of being productive and/or feeling important than with getting strong business results. Without realizing it, they spend more time getting their emotional needs met than building successful businesses.

Chapter 10

High Heels in a World of Oxfords

As we approached the conference hall, it looked like every other one that I had visited that year. It was my first time speaking at this location and yet everything seemed eerily the same, There was a cold stone exterior on the building with a few splashes of color here and there. Lawns were trimmed, windows cleaned, and two greeters stationed at the front door awaiting my arrival. They had been instructed to greet the guest speakers, provide light refreshments, and then show them to their special seats in the front row. It was so "pro forma" that it was almost sterile!

My associate and I got out of the car and began the ritual of gathering the CDs, pamphlets, and books for our product table. There were only a few bags, so between our four hands, we could manage everything. We had that down to a science!

As if on cue, our assigned greeters left their doorway perch and headed to our vehicle. I chuckled softly to myself, knowing what would happen next. "Can we take those bags for you?" they asked. I smiled as my associate started to object and then resigned himself to the surrender of our supplies. Our attentive greeters brought us inside and assured us that our promotions table would be set up, PowerPoint slides given to the tech booth, and handouts placed safely in the hands of the ushers, who would await further instructions.

The speakers' room was on an upper level and was quite nice. Small bottles of assorted beverages and a variety of bagged snacks were spread out on a welcome table. There were some comfortable chairs within which to relax and catch a quick breath before presenting. After hearing that my associate preferred coffee, a cup was specially brewed to meet his needs. Within a few minutes we headed downstairs for the seminar. As we walked through the crowd of mostly strangers, smiling and nodding through our procession, we would be stopped occasionally so my associate could be introduced to some friends.

As we reached the front row, I sat down next to my associate for whom they had provided a tall name-brand bottle of water. They obviously felt he would be exerting enough effort this evening to require such substantial hydration. In their minds, they had thought of everything!

Across the room, I spotted some friends and walked over for a quick embrace. Actually, they were the only reason we had come. This was their sphere of influence and they had felt the timing was right for my message to be presented. After a quick hug, I scooted back to my seat. The music was already playing and they were ready to begin.

They called my associate and me to the platform, and as he greeted the people, I triple-checked that my iPad was cued to the first slide of my presentation. As he turned and handed the microphone to me and sat down, I watched with amusement as confusion rippled through the crowd. A woman? It was the woman who was the financial planner and guest speaker? I smiled and winked at our greeters who had faithfully waited on my associate upstairs, attending to his every need while I sat reading my notes beside him.

I did that because I wanted to assure them that I was not offended. They had no idea how many times I had relived that scenario; while I was speaking in a different place this time, it was the same experience!

Regardless of the setting, the role of a woman in the business world still lacks acceptable definition. It is still being shaped, so it will take time for it to be clearly delineated and fully accepted. Cultural change requires people change, which can take time. The ingrained assumption is that it will always be the man who steps forward and speaks. He is the "keeper of the business realm," and he alone holds the keys to unlock wisdom and wealth. While his abilities in the business realm are deserving of acknowledgement and his contributions in the areas of business development are undisputed, males are hardly the only significant players on the field.

As women we cannot wait for society to acknowledge us before we stand up and assert ourselves in the marketplace. We must walk in the confidence of who we are and boldly advance into the business realm.

The traditional view of a woman's skill sets as adequate only for maternal, marital, or other familial purposes has significantly limited her opportunities for self-expression and self-fulfillment. Even though she could make substantive contributions in many other spheres of activity, she has been largely constrained in doing so. This traditional view does not acknowledge all that she is capable of nor the fullness of her identity. Her ability to birth, nurture, and create is not limited to familial activities. To the contrary, her innate capabilities enable her to take a business or personal dream and transition it to a robust vision. Once her CEO DNA codes are uncovered and released, she can literally birth, nurture, and cultivate new dimensions of life for herself, which may include one or more business empires. This gifting and innate capability should not be overlooked, denigrated, or silenced. Rather, it is time for the marketplace to embrace women as multifaceted leaders with the ability to birth, create, and bring to fruition.

As women we cannot wait for society to acknowledge us before we stand up and assert ourselves in the marketplace. We must walk in the confidence of who we are and boldly advance into the business realm.

However, such advancement requires a carefully constructed strategy.

According to *Webster's* dictionary, "advancement" includes the following definitions:

(1) The science and art of employing the political, economic, psychological, and military forces of a nation or group of nations to afford the maximum support to adopted policies in peace or war.
(2) The science and art of military command exercised to meet the enemy in combat under advantageous conditions.

Notice that in the first definition, they list four different areas that must be pulled together to support a goal— those areas being: political, economic, psychological, and military. In the second definition, it explains that the purpose for all these areas being pulled together is to make sure that every interaction is advantageous...or in other words—nothing is wasted and it all can be used to achieve a specific goal.

Having a strategy is essential if we are to have a plan that pulls all of our resources together to ensure the realization of our goals. Too many times we focus on some tactical tool or process with which we feel comfortable and call that our strategy. That is self-deception. Tools and other tactical activities are important, but only as they are used to support an overall, all-encompassing strategy.

In the business realm, our success as business owners and highly compensated employees relies upon our commitment to awaken and sharpen the CEO DNA Codes within us and use them as tools to implement the strategies we have devised.

Developing the CEO Code of Administration

Administration in the business realm is about as critical as breathing. Things do not go well without it! It is the ability to see the entire scope of a given situation, envision a solution, and then create a plan that brings closure. Administration requires thought and attention to detail. The ability to focus and refocus between macro to micro observations is essential. Women do that in the home every hour of every day! This is an innate skill that we have. Lucky you! Lucky me! Lucky us!

The ability to focus and refocus between macro to micro observations is essential. Women do that in the home every hour of every day!

One of the first steps in building Crystal Clear Finances was to create the vision of a comprehensive financial planning office, identifying in detail what it would physically, emotionally, and financially look like. Although I had no clients at the time, I began to draft a procedure entitled, "The Perfect Client Experience." I outlined the goal of what I wanted each potential client to experience from the moment they contacted my office until they became clients. I even took it one step further and wrote a policy stating the services that would be provided to appreciate them and retain them as clientele.

I also created a written procedure that outlined a process that would take someone from prospect to customer to "fan!" In order to accomplish this, I needed to look at things through their eyes to understand their experience in working with our office. Was it hard to do business with us in any way? Did they have trouble connecting with us or finding me? I gathered all the information that I could, and laid out a plan to remove any obstacle I found.

Too often we presume that our clients just want strong returns from their investments. That is certainly true, but much too simplistic. They want financial success, but they also want to have that happen in a way that is emotionally satisfying. Every transaction needs to meet a business need but in a way that is personally fulfilling.

I agree with the person who said that people may not remember what you said, or what you did, but they will always remember how you made them feel. I took time to determine the ideal process for client follow-through once we had our introductory meeting. I made note of the results of our discussion and what they should experience next. Why did I do this? I wanted to create fans—enthusiastic promoters—of Crystal Clear Finances by anticipating their needs in advance and otherwise serving them in a manner that exceeded all of their expectations.

I took the objective for each subsequent interaction and devised a process that would consistently fulfill not only my client's expectations, but my own. These processes became the operational guidelines for each division in our office. I now had the means to measure our performance so I could ensure complete client satisfaction on an ongoing basis.

There have been times when we have experienced an influx of abundance for no apparent reason. Some people call it "having a good month" or just "that time of year." However, I don't believe in luck or that things "just happen." I believe in the principle that "what you sow, you reap." So if there is client activity beyond the typical business ebb and flow, I feel it is a direct result of some effort, some tool, or some procedure that was successfully implemented. Wisdom requires that you be able to identify the cause of business shifts so that you can reinforce the changes that brought unusually good results or correct the problems that caused a downward trend.

Good administration requires the effective use of performance metrics. There are a variety of tools and protocols that can be used and they do not have to be complicated to be effective. In our office, one of the measurement tools we use is a simple form that lists all prospects and client meetings for the month. On this form we indicate whether a client is new, and if so, where they heard about us. At the end of the month, I review this form with my administration team so we can see what we were doing to bring new clients to our office. Our level of measurement is so precise that we can tell which of our radio stations most of our clients are dialing in and when!

This is helpful in times of positive growth, but essential in times when we see a downward shift in appointments. We can check the form to see how our topics or commercials have changed and determine the immediate effect those changes have had on our listeners.

This information, positive or negative, is evaluated to make sure we fully understand how our actions are affecting our business results. Whenever we have a deviation in expected results, we step back and reexamine both our strategy and supporting tactics to ensure we are doing the right things.

As women in the workplace, we can choose the level of excellence within which we desire to operate. There are plenty of people, male and female, who are content to stagnate at some point in their lives, such as in a place of employment. They are content to park there, with no inner desire to excel. That is such a tragedy. However, I do not believe that applies to you, dear reader. You would not be reading this if you were content to stay where you are!

As women in the workplace, we can choose the level of excellence within which we desire to operate.

I challenge you who desire to become HCEs (Highly Compensated Employees) and/or business owners, to move past your status quo and begin to energize your unique "Code of Administration" so that you can realize your dreams and have the life you have always wanted.

Code of Operations in Business

Once you have identified your expectations and have used administration to write down your goals and outline the steps you need to achieve them, it is time for operations to begin.

Operations is taking the plan that is on paper and bringing it to life. It is the active, physical pursuit of your goals, the breathing of life into your dreams, and the building of momentum day by day. The code of operations allows you to work your plan and make it happen!

In my office, I play a key role in operations. I understand and embody the vision of Crystal Clear Finances, but I also have a concrete, down-to-earth description of how to implement the plan. I provide one-on-one consultations with potential clients with the intention of helping them become clients of Crystal Clear Finances. That may not sound glamorous or exciting, but it is the physical action that is required to bring the vision into reality.

Early in my career, operations was one of the key areas in which I struggled prioritizing my activities and managing my time. There were so many urgent tasks to complete that I felt overwhelmed by all the responsibilities required to build and grow my business. I made the mistake of trying to do everything for everyone. Instead of identifying the specific CEO DNA Codes for administration, operations, sales/marketing, and finance, I placed them all in one jumbled bag of responsibilities. The mere fact that it needed to be done and that I had the skill set to complete it qualified them to be placed on my ever-growing task list. This fundamental problem was a lack of delegation of most of those tasks. I had become a one-woman show. That was painful to experience, and, no doubt, painfully unpleasant to watch!

I surveyed the lists created through administration and began an assessment of the tasks that only I could perform. All others were to be delegated immediately. Through this experience it became clear that just because I am capable to do something, does not mean I should be the one to do it!

It was only when I realized that I possessed these Codes and could deploy them to my advantage that mental clarity began to push back the cloud of confusion and despair. I surveyed the lists created through administration and began an assessment of the tasks that only I could perform. All others were to be delegated immediately. Through this experience it became clear that just because I am capable to do something, does not mean I should be the one to do it!

There are many books that teach extensively about time management, so I am sure many have heard of the Pareto 80/20 rule. It states that 20 percent of your activities are typically sufficient to support 80 percent of your business. Similarly, if you focused on just the top 20 percent of your clients, you would probably achieve 80 percent of your business objectives. This is due to the fact that much of the time we spend is in areas that don't have the potential to provide real results. Essentially, we major on the minors.

Now, let's take that 80/20 concept just one step further and look at Pareto "squared." Take those twenty issues that have the most potential and whittle them down until you are left with only the most significant and promising four. Focus your attention on these and you will see some serious results. In some respects, these should be the only things that receive your attention. That is not possible in the real world, but any activities that diminish your focus on those high-return items should be minimized.

If you could focus on these top four items exclusively, Pareto's Rule would indicate that your productivity should increase by another 64 percent. The irony is that by lowering the number of things you do in order to focus on just a few critical items, you greatly increase your productivity!

You could literally take the game plan presented by Administration and then implement it with a 64 percent productivity increase! This is a dramatic example of why it is so important to measure and understand the results of our actions. We can switch from just being active and running from one crisis to another, to focusing on the most important and promising activities. If we need to develop our skills to be more effective in those areas, then we should do so, for it will provide the results and satisfaction we need.

Implementing the Code of Sales/Marketing in the Work Environment

Have you ever walked into a room and felt overdressed? How about showing up with the same outfit as another individual in the room? Talk about a fashion faux pas!

I have been to conferences where the suggested attire was business casual and found myself significantly overdressed, with nothing in my hotel room to remedy the situation. What I would have given to have known the environment that I was stepping into and how to prepare for it!

**Marketing allows us to take vision
and articulate it in a manner that is easily understood.
Our communications should be so effective that it
doesn't require our audience to think!**

Sales/marketing provides understanding of the environment you are entering and awareness of the self-generated atmosphere that you are bringing with you. It is all about understanding your audience and their level of understanding so that you can effectively communicate your critical messages. Marketing allows us to take vision and articulate it in a manner that is easily understood. Our communications should be so effective that it doesn't require our audience to think! If they have to think about what we are saying in order to decipher it, we have failed. When deciding on the messaging that you will present to a given audience, factor in their level of understanding, and don't make them think!

I work with many pre-retirees, and understanding their individual needs is essential to proper financial planning.

However, finances aren't the only issue causing enormous stress to this particular group.

Studies have shown that pre-retirees experience five phases as they walk through the transition from pre-retiree to retiree, Only one of those phases deals with finance! They will experience the joy of leaving a job, the fear of not having enough, the loss of identity, and despondency due to displacement, before they finally reengage. Each of these stages occur at different times and for different durations. In spite of the fact that it happens to millions of pre-retirees across this nation every year, few are aware of what is happening.

Effective and compassionate marketing requires a comprehensive understanding of a given audience, so that we can tailor our message to address their concerns, and present our solutions in a manner that is easily understood.

Why is this important for our office to know? Because effective and compassionate marketing requires a comprehensive understanding of a given audience, so that we can tailor our message to address their concerns, and present our solutions in a manner that is easily understood.

Sales/marketing in the business realm has often been about positioning for a quick, short-term sale. That is really tragic, as modest short-term gain can preclude long-term relationships with strong long-term profit. It pays to care. It pays to be real. It pays to know the needs that your customers have and provide genuine, cost-effective solutions.

This will require work. You will need to have an understanding of your demographic groups, their needs, their emotions, and the solutions for which they are searching. All this requires that you not only study them, but that you also study yourself. You will need to know your message, and be passionate about it. Your mission must be clear and unmistakable. Your mission cannot be just something memorialized on some plaque on the wall. It has to be part of your DNA fiber so that you, yourself, become the marketing tool. Only then will you embody the essence of the character for your business or place of employment.

I remember meeting with the CEO of a company to review the financial recommendation that I had prepared for his organization. We were friends and he was pleased with the advice I had given. His last request before implementation was that I meet with his board of directors before they wrote the check. I was happy to oblige. I spent time before the meeting preparing, reviewing all my documentation and financial projections. I felt confident that I could explain the overall strategy for my recommendation. The meeting went smoothly and everything ran as planned. I had crossed my "t's" and dotted my "i's." Then they asked one final question: "Why should we do business with you?"

I calmly explained that I operated with integrity and I was well versed in my field. I showed my credentials, which were twice as long and significantly more impressive than the average planner. Yet, they said there were others who could match my skill set and operated with integrity. I could feel the sweat begin to surface and trickle down my back as they continued to press me for an answer of distinction. I closed my eyes and dug back to the core of why I had started my business, and then passionately explained that it wasn't about building the biggest financial planning office. It was not that I would be the only one with integrity or credentials in my field, for I knew those were just tools. The reason I had started Crystal Clear Finances and the reason I felt they should engage me was because I had come to a place where I was tired of men and women barely having two nickels to rub together. I was tired of women thinking they did not possess the intelligence or the authority to operate within their ingrained CEO Codes and become successful. I had dedicated my life to empowering individuals to understand the realm of finances and take their rightful position within it. I was building a business that would provide a voice to women and the financial substance to turn dreams into realities. If they believed that this was the type of organization that they wanted to support, then they should invest with me.

The room was silent, my sweat was now more than a trickle, and my mouth was dry from my impassioned delivery, but slowly they began to smile and lean back in their chairs. I knew then that they had heard my message.

You must have a message that is uniquely your own. This message must infiltrate every area of your marketing. People will engage in business with you because they want to. Their minds will always justify what their hearts want. Therefore, you will need to ensure that your heart connects with their heart in a genuine, transparent way.

Once you understand your message, have fun and be creative! Understand that you are not limited to a few over-used marketing tools or traditional ways of fabricating and presenting your thoughts. To the contrary, you have access to the entire spectrum of communications. For example, social media has opened an entirely new avenue of communication through Facebook, Twitter, Google, blogging, websites, and the list goes on! Part of unlocking the CEO Codes within you requires the study and application of areas that you have not ventured into before!

Set in Place the CEO Code of Finance

Measuring the results of our actions is not only critical for the CEO DNA Codes of administration, operations, and marketing, but it is also essential in the realm of "finances." Finances are the lifeblood of any organization. They sustain daily operations that incrementally achieve the original business vision, while providing a platform for continued expansion.

Sales help transition curious prospects into established clients. The net results are the purchase of goods and/or services. Knowing the cost of each product you offer or service you provide can ensure that your sales generate the appropriate profit margins.

As you start a business or assume a role of financial management, you need to evaluate your current financial position.

As you start a business or assume a role of financial management, you need to evaluate your current financial position. Learn to effectively understand the "Profit and Loss Statement" and "Balance Sheet" of your company. This does not mean that you must become a Certified Financial Planner™, but it does mean you need to be aware of your cash flow, your operating expenses, and your profitability on a regular basis. I review my expenses weekly, and on a monthly basis, I compare them to my current and previous years' budgets. This helps to highlight areas where expenses may be increasing unnecessarily, and allows me to take immediate action to protect the financial foundations of the business.

It is important that you create a "war chest" for the future expansion of your enterprise. This can only happen by effectively managing the funds that enter and leave your business on a daily basis. Don't buy into the lie that it is a "business tax write-off," as an excuse to purchase whatever you want. Learn to be strategic in all purchases and business investments. Be alert to the slightest dependence on debt and become skillful in understanding the difference between debt and leverage. Dependence on debt is a two-edged sword. It can help you bridge cash flow gaps, but it can also grow to the point that it destroys the business. On the other hand, leverage can be used to position for advancement and therefore represents an investment in the future as opposed to daily operations.

Dependence on debt is a two-edged sword. It can help you bridge cash flow gaps, but it can also grow to the point that it destroys the business.

I've met many business owners whose natural skill sets were skewed towards administration, operations, or sales/marketing, with little interest in the financial aspects of their businesses. This is especially common among women business owners who claim that finances are just not their "thing." This excuse has led to many business failures and no small amount of personal and familial stress. Although you can hire someone to do the day-to-day administration of finances, business owners cannot be excused from the responsibility of financial accountability. Employees can help you run the numbers, but you must understand and evaluate the results. Forfeiting this responsibility is a death sentence for any business.

> **We can and must focus on our primary skill set, but not at the expense of closing our eyes to the financial side of our businesses.**

I mentioned previously that I had a doctor who came to me on the brink of bankruptcy. He explained that he had spent years in medical school and learned all about the human body and how to facilitate healing. Upon completing his residency, he was hundreds of thousands of dollars in debt. He proceeded to join with other doctors and they started their own clinic. All of them were extremely skilled in their abilities and the demand for their services grew. Yet, here he sat, a brilliant doctor whose hands had brought life and overcome death, but now he was being forced to close his practice because he had nothing with which to pay his staff or keep his building.

I asked the physician about his billing procedures and financial statements, and he replied that he was a doctor— not a financial planner, and that in all his years in medical school they never taught him how to effectively run a business; they only taught him to heal, and unfortunately, that wasn't enough. We can and must focus on our primary skill set, but not at the expense of closing our eyes to the financial side of our businesses.

As a businesswoman, it is up to you to decide the strength that you will bring to a company. Cultivating your CEO DNA Codes of administration, operations, sales/marketing, and finance can effectively launch and establish you as a vibrant leader within the business community.

Ask Yourself...

1. Are you confident enough to laugh at outdated perceptions regarding the role of a woman?

2. Are you willing to push the envelope and bring needed
changes to your sphere of influence?

3. Are you intentional in your thought process as to how
you will implement change around you?

4. What CEO DNA Codes do you see in full operation at
home, the workplace, and your community?

5. Do you carry your own message?

Final Word

One Woman to Another

As women, we have a unique opportunity to shape our world by unlocking our innate CEO DNA Codes. We can open doors, remove stumbling blocks, and set strong foundations for our daughters, granddaughters, sisters, and various women within our spheres. History will record that we were the ones who unleashed the unmistakable roar of real femininity, leaving an indelible impact on our society, and redefining our cultural influence!

Embrace your femininity! Give yourself permission to discover, celebrate, and enjoy who you are. Refuse any notion that you are second-class or inferior in any way. You have nothing to prove; no endorsements from the male gender are required. You can simply be…you!

In regards to the CEO DNA Codes that are within you, don't worry about creating them; they are already there! Rather, take the time to discover and cultivate them, for those Codes carry within them the seeds of your provision, advancement, and fulfillment.

Each of us enters this CEO DNA revelation at different stages in our lives. Do not let this concern you; this is not a competition. We are all in this together!

Regardless of your season in life or your socioeconomic status, it is never too late to unlock your inner codes to experience your own individual growth or to enhance the lives of wandering "cubs" in need of a "Mama Bear" to invest in them!

You have permission to color outside the lines. You can be the real you! You are no longer a captive to restrictive thoughts and role definitions. You will make mistakes along the way, but we all do. So, big deal! Welcome to the human race! In time, and with practice, your mistakes will become fewer and farther between. Just persevere!

Above all, never betray your femininity in order to be accepted by others. Set your own standards. Be successful, by your design, and others will inevitably benefit.

Keep the Curls.

Cultivate your CEO DNA Codes.

Create your Culture.

About the Author

Crystal Langdon is a Certified Financial Planner™ and Registered Investment Advisor. She is an author, gifted national motivational speaker, and radio talk show host. She has created and presented numerous life-changing investment seminars. Crystal believes it is time for women of all ages to understand the incredible power that is already within them, power that can lead to great personal and professional success.

Learn more about Crystal Langdon at

www.Crystalclearfinances.com or

Keepthecurlsbook.com